*Hiro Sachiya
Talks about
Japanese Religion*

装丁 ───────── スタジオ・ギブ（川島 進）
装画 ───────── 小森哲郎
　　　　　　　　牛乗り天神（米沢・相良人形）
イラストレーション ───── 田中忠宏

本文デザイン ──────── 戸村裕子

Published by Japan Book Inc.
3-17-85 Akitsucho, Higashi-Murayama City, Tokyo 189-0001
No part of this publication may be reproduced in any form or
by any means without permission in writing from the publisher.
Copyright © 2010 by Hiro Sachiya, James M. Vardaman
All right reserved. Printed in Japan.

First Edition 2010

ひろさちやの
英語で話す
日本の宗教Q&A

Hiro Sachiya Talks about Japanese Religion

Hiro Sachiya
ひろさちや [著]

James.M.Vardaman
ジェームス・M・バーダマン [訳]

Japan**B**ook

目次

序章	日本人は無宗教なのか	6
第1章	太古 はじめに神様がいた	20
第2章	飛鳥―奈良時代 仏教が日本にやってきた	50
第3章	平安時代 輸入仏教から国産仏教へ	74
第4章	鎌倉時代 民衆仏教の成立と展開	112
第5章	室町時代 キリスト教がやってきた	148
第6章	江戸時代 仏教が骨抜きにされた	164
第7章	近代 おかしな宗教が捏造された	186
終章	日本人は宗教アレルギー	202

CONTENTS

INTRODUCTION — 7
Are the Japanese Irreligious?

CHAPTER 1   ANCIENT TIMES — 21
First There Were the Gods

CHAPTER 2   ASUKA–NARA PERIOD — 51
Buddhism Arrives in Japan

CHAPTER 3   HEIAN PERIOD — 75
From Imported Buddhism to Buddhism Made in Japan

CHAPTER 4   KAMAKURA PERIOD — 113
The Formation and Development of Popular Buddhism

CHAPTER 5   MUROMACHI PERIOD — 149
Christianity Arrives

CHAPTER 6   EDO PERIOD — 165
Buddhism Rendered Powerless

CHAPTER 7   MODERN TIMES — 187
Strange Religions are Concocted

FINAL CHAPTER — 203
The Japanese Religious Allergy

序章

日本人は無宗教なのか

 日本人は無宗教だと言われています。
本当ですか？

　　最初からむずかしい質問ですね。この質問に答えるには、まず「宗教」がどういうものであるかが明らかにされる必要があります。

　じつは、キリスト教にしてもユダヤ教にしても、またイスラム教にしても、それらの宗教は「契約一神教」と呼ばれるべきものなんです。これは、ただ一つの神を選んで、

「わたしはあなただけを唯一絶対の神と信じ、他の神は認めません」

といって、その唯一絶対の神と契約を結びます。

　この唯一絶対の存在は、キリスト教ではゴッド、ユダヤ教ではヤハウェ、イスラム教だとアッラーですが、信者というのは神と契約を結んでいるのですから、自分が信者であるか否かがはっきりしています。

　けれども、日本人にとっての神は、それとはまったく違った存在です。日本では昔から「八百万の神」と呼ばれているほど、まことに神々の数が多い。八百万も神々がいれば、とてもとても全部の神と契約を結ぶことができません。

INTRODUCTION

Are the Japanese Irreligious?

> **It is said that Japanese do not believe in any religion. Is that really true?**

This is a difficult question to start off with. In order to answer it, we first have to make clear what we mean by "religion."

As it happens, when it comes to Christianity, Judaism or Islam, each is what should be called "covenant monotheism." That is, each selects one single god, saying "I believe you are the one-and-only, absolute god and recognize no other gods," and enters into a covenant with that one-and-only, absolute god.

This single, absolute being is called God in Christianity, Yahweh in Judaism and Allah in Islam, and a believer is one who enters into a covenant with a specific god, so it is very clear whether a person is a believer or not.

To the Japanese, however, a god is an entirely different entity. In Japan, from ancient times, it has been said that there are so many gods that they are countless, "myriads of gods and deities." If there are countless gods, then it is completely impossible to enter into a covenant with all of them.

それじゃあ、代表的な神を選んで、その神とだけ契約を結べばいいじゃないかと言われそうですが、ある神だけを選んで拝むと、場合によれば他の神々から嫉妬を受けます。だから、特定の神とだけ契約を結んではいけない。日本人の宗教はそういう宗教なんです。

　それで、キリスト教、ユダヤ教、イスラム教のほうから見れば、日本人は無宗教のように見えるのでしょうね。また、日本人自身も、日本の宗教は一神教とは根本的に構造が違っているもので、「どうやらわたしは無宗教なんだ」と思ってしまうようです。

 いま「日本の宗教」と言われましたが、それは神道ですか？　それとも仏教？

　日本の宗教、あるいは日本人の宗教は、仏教ではありません。

　一般には、日本は仏教国だとされています。しかし、なるほど日本に仏教は伝来しましたが、日本人は伝来した仏教を完膚なきまでに変形してしまい、現在日本にある仏教はもはや「仏教」という名では呼べない代物になってしまっています。

　したがって、日本を仏教国と呼ぶことはできないでしょう。なお、仏教が仏教ならざるものに変容するプロセスは、われわれは本書の第2章以下で詳しく検討することにします。

Well then, why not choose a representative god and enter into a covenant with just that god? If you choose only one god and worship it, however, that might just arouse the jealousy of the other gods. Therefore, you cannot enter into a covenant with just one specific god. Japanese religion is that sort of religion.

That is why, from the viewpoint of Christianity, Judaism and Islam, Japanese appear to have no religion. So, even the Japanese end up thinking, because the religion of the Japanese is fundamentally different in makeup from monotheism, "Apparently we are unbelievers."

You just mentioned "the religion of the Japanese," but does that mean Shintō, or Buddhism?

The religion of Japan—the religion of the Japanese—is not Buddhism.

However, in general, Japan is considered a Buddhist country. To be sure, Buddhism was introduced into Japan, but the Japanese people transformed it thoroughly, and the Buddhism that is found in Japan today is a substitute that cannot really be called "Buddhism" in a proper sense of the term.

As a result, Japan cannot be called a "Buddhist country." Further, we will consider in chapter two and thereafter the process by which Buddhism transformed into something unlike Buddhism.

 **では、日本の宗教は仏教ではないとして、それは神道でしょうか？**

　その問いに対しては、「イエス」でもって答えるべきでしょう。だが、それでは、神道とは何かと問われるなら、これがまたややこしいのです。われわれは第1章で「神道とは何か？」を考察することにしますが、少し先回りして語るなら、
　――神道とは日本人の宗教である――
となります。とすると、主語と述語を入れ換えれば、これは、
　――日本人の宗教は神道である――
ということになります。それだと何も言っていないのと同じですね。
　まあ、ともかく、日本の宗教は神道です。そこに6世紀に日本に仏教が伝来して、仏教が日本の宗教、文化に大きな影響を及ぼしました。仏教が日本の宗教、文化に大きな刺激と影響を与えたことは否定できませんが、仏教そのものは完全に日本化されてしまい――日本化されたということは神道化されたということと同義です――形骸化し、ある意味では消滅してしまいました。
　一方、神道のほうも仏教から大きな影響を受けて、本来の神道から大きく変わってしまいました。したがって、ある意味では、日本の宗教は神道と仏教がミックスされたものと言うべきかもしれません。それを宗教学者は、
　――神仏習合あるいは神仏混淆――
と呼んでいます。だが、わたしはそれをあえて神道だと言いたいのです。
　それからもう一つ、明治以後の日本においては

All right then, if Buddhism is not "the religion of Japan," does that mean it is Shintoism?

In response to that, one should probably answer "yes." But in doing so, if you are asked what Shintō is, that is another complicated issue. We will consider "What is Shintoism?" in chapter one, but to go ahead and give the answer, "Shintō is the religion of the Japanese people." Or, if we switch the subject and the predicate, "The religion of the Japanese people is Shintoism." Saying that is the same as saying nothing.

Anyway, the religion of Japan is Shintoism. Then, in the 6th century, Buddhism was introduced to Japan and it had a major influence on Japanese religion and culture. It is impossible to deny that Buddhism stimulated and had a far-reaching influence upon Japanese religion and culture. But Buddhism itself ended up completely Japanized (Japanized means the same thing as "becoming Shintō in character"), turning into an empty shell, and in a sense disappearing.

On the other hand, Shintō was greatly influenced by Buddhism, and it ended up being greatly changed from what it originally was. As a result, in one sense perhaps one ought to say that Japanese religion became a mix of Shintoism and Buddhism. Scholars of religion call this the syncretic fusion of Shintoism and Buddhism (*shinbutsu shūgō*) or the mixture of Buddhism and Shintoism (*shinbutsu konkō*). But I venture to say that this is Shintoism.

For another thing, a *fake* religion called "State Shintoism"

INTRODUCTION   11

「国家神道」と呼ばれるニセモノ宗教がつくられ、1945（昭和20）年の日本の敗戦にいたるまでそれが国民に強制され、国民を支配しました。

「国家神道」というのは、立憲君主にすぎない天皇を、人間ではなしに「現人神」（人の姿となってこの世に出現した神）であると権力でもって国民に強制的に信じさせ、崇拝させる擬似宗教です。そうすることによって、国民をして国家への忠誠心を持たせ、国家に隷属させることが目的でした。

このような擬似宗教・ニセモノ宗教を強制的に信じさせられたもので、日本人はそのような「国家神道」に対して嫌悪感を抱き、ひいては宗教嫌いになりました。日本人が無宗教だと言われる背景には、このような「国家神道」への反発があります。日本人は宗教アレルギーだと言ってよいでしょう。

ですから、わたしは「神道」といった言葉をあまり使いたくありません。そこで、わたしは日本の宗教を「やまと教」と呼んでいます。"やまと"は日本国の異称です。したがって、「やまと教」というのは、日本人の宗教だということになります。

では、いったい宗教とは何なのですか……？

宗教とは何か？　じつは、宗教学者の数だけ宗教の定義があると言われているほど、宗教を定義することはむずかしいのです。世界にはさまざまな宗教があります。神の存在を認める宗教もあれば、神の存在を認めない宗教もあります。また、その神も、多神教といって多数の神の存在を認めるものもある

was created in Japan following Meiji, and until Japan's defeat in war in 1945, this was forced upon the people and it controlled them.

State Shintoism was a pseudo-religion in which authority forced the Japanese people to believe that the emperor, who is no more than the constitutional sovereign, is not a human being but "a living god" (*arahitogami*), a deity manifested in this world in the form of a human being. Its purpose in doing this was to make the people loyal to the state and put them under the state's control.

Because they were forced to believe in this fake religion, Japanese harbored a dislike for "State Shintoism," and by extension, came to dislike religion in general. In the background of Japanese being pictured as having no religion is this resistance to "State Shintoism." One could even say that Japanese are "allergic" to religion.

For that reason, I would prefer not to use the word "Shintō." Instead, I prefer to call the religion of Japan "Yamatoism" (*Yamatokyō*). "Yamato" is another name for Japan. Therefore, "Yamatoism" is the religion of the Japanese people.

In that case, just what is "religion"?

What is religion? The truth of the matter is, there are as many definitions of religion as there are scholars of religion. That is how hard it is to define religion. Among the various religions in the world, some recognize the existence of a divine being, while others do not. Further, some religions, called polytheistic religions, recognize the existence of a great number of gods,

し、神は唯一絶対の存在だとする宗教もあります。すべての宗教に共通する共通点は、なかなか見つかりません。

　そこでわたしは、本書においては、宗教を簡単に、

　　――人間らしい生き方を教えるもの――

と定義しておきます。学問的には不完全な定義かもしれませんが、本書は学術書ではありませんから、いちおうこれで十分だと思います。

　さて、ここでちょっとキリスト教の開祖のイエスの言葉を引用します。イエスは『新約聖書』の中で、

　　《あなたがたも聞いているとおり、「目には目を、歯には歯を」と命じられている。しかし、わたしは言っておく。悪人に手向かってはならない。だれかがあなたの右の頬（ほお）を打つなら、左の頬を向けなさい》（「マタイによる福音書（ふくいんしょ）」）

と言っています。ここで「目には目を、歯には歯を」と言われているのは、じつはユダヤ教の律法（りっぽう）です。ユダヤ教においては、自分の目が潰（つぶ）されたら相手の目を潰してよい、と教えています。歯を折られれば相手の歯を折ってよいのです。

　しかし、歯を折られて相手の命まで奪ってはいけません。それは拡大報復になります。「目には目を、歯には歯を」は同害報復（どうがいほうふく）を言っているのです。

　そして、ユダヤ教は民族宗教です。ユダヤ教の神（ヤハウェ）は、ただユダヤ人だけの神であり、ユダヤ人だけを救います。

　イエスは、その考え方を否定しました。神は全人類の神であり、全人類を救われるのだと主張しまし

while other religions, called monotheistic religions, believe that there is only one god and that god is absolute. It is exceedingly difficult to find common features shared by all religions.

Therefore, in this volume, I define religion in very plain terms as "something that teaches people how to live in a way that befits human beings." In academic terms, this may be an inadequate definition, but then, this book is not an academic work, and for the present I believe that definition is adequate.

Now I would like to quote from Jesus, the founder of Christianity. According to the Gospel according to St. Matthew, in the New Testament of the Bible, Jesus said:

> You have heard that they were told, 'Eye for eye, tooth for tooth.' But what I tell you is this: Do not set yourself against the man who wrongs you. If someone slaps you on the right cheek, turn and offer him your left. *Matthew* 5:38

The phrase "eye for eye, tooth for tooth" is actually from the laws of Judaism. Within Judaic belief, it is taught that if one's eye is destroyed by another person, it is acceptable to destroy that person's eye in return. If one has his tooth broken by someone, one can break that person's tooth in return.

However, if one's tooth is broken off, one is not allowed to take that person's life. That becomes an escalation of retaliation. "An eye for an eye, a tooth for a tooth" means retaliation of the same degree.

Judaism is a folk religion. The god of Judaism—Yahweh—is the god of only the Jews, and only Jews can be saved.

Jesus rejected that way of thinking. He held that God is the god of all humanity, and that all humanity can be saved.

た。それで、ユダヤ教の「目には目を」の考え方を否定し、加害者に対する報復ではなしに「愛」を説いたのです。それがキリスト教です。つまりキリスト教は、ユダヤ人といった狭い民族の枠を超えて、普遍的な人間としての生き方を教えています。

　そこで、ユダヤ教が民族宗教であるのに対して、キリスト教・イスラム教・仏教は普遍宗教(世界宗教ともいいます)です。
　以上でお分かりのように、宗教には、
　──民族宗教と普遍宗教──
の二つがあります。そして普遍宗教は普遍的な人間としての生き方を教えているのに対して、民族宗教はそれぞれの民族としての生き方を教えています。ユダヤ教はユダヤ人としての生き方を教えているのです。また、やまと教は日本の民族宗教ですから、日本人としての生き方を教えています。
　しかしながら、同じ民族宗教であっても、ユダヤ教とやまと教には大きな違いがあります。

　ユダヤ教では成文法の形式でもって律法(生き方)が示されているのに対し、やまと教では不文法(慣習法)の形式で生き方が教えられています。不文法・慣習法はあまり強制力を持ちません。
　それに現在の日本の社会は利害の対立する集団でもって構成されていますから、一つにまとまることなくバラバラになっています。それゆえ民族宗教であるやまと教の影響力が稀薄になっています。そのために日本人が無宗教であると思われてしまうのではないでしょうか。

Therefore, he denied the teaching of "an eye for an eye" in Judaism and preached "love," not retaliation, toward those who inflict harm. That is what Christianity is all about. In other words, Christianity goes beyond the narrow bounds of the folkways of the Jewish people and teaches a universal view of how a human being should live.

From that view, while Judaism is a folk religion, Christianity, Islam and Buddhism are universalistic religions (also called a world religions).

As can be seen from the above, there are two kinds of religion: folk religions and universalistic religions. While the universalistic religions teach how a universalistic human being should live, folk religions teach the various folk how they should live. Judaism teaches how the Jewish person should live. Likewise, Yamatoism, as the folk religion of Japan, teaches how one should live *as a Japanese*.

That having been said, even though they are both folk religions, there is a major difference between Judaism and Yamatoism.

Whereas Judaism teaches its rules (how to live) through the form of written laws, Yamatoism teaches its own rules for living through unwritten laws. Unwritten, customary laws do not possess much force.

And because present-day Japanese society is composed of groups whose interests clash with those of others, these rules are left inconsistent and disorganized. Accordingly, the influence of Yamatoism, because it is a folk religion, is watered down. This is probably why the Japanese are thought to not have a religion.

INTRODUCTION   17

 **❺ なぜ日本人は、結婚式を神道式でやり、葬式を仏教式でやるのですか？**

　結婚式も葬式も、要するに習俗です。日本人は、葬式をするのが宗教だと思っていますが大まちがいです。それが証拠に、宗教を否定した社会主義国においても、葬式や結婚式はあります。

　宗教の仕事は、人間らしい生き方を教えることですよ。葬式をお坊さんがやるのは、あれはアルバイト（副業）だと思ってください。しかし、現代の日本では、本業を忘れてアルバイトばかりしている宗教家が多すぎますね。

Why do Japanese have Shintō wedding ceremonies and Buddhism funeral ceremonies?

Weddings and funerals are, in short, folkways. The Japanese think that holding a funeral is religion, but that is a major mistake. As evidence for this, notice that even in earlier socialist countries which had rejected religion entirely there were funerals and weddings.

The work of religion is to teach how one should live as a human being. When a priest performs a funeral ceremony, please think of it as a part-time job, a form of secondary employment. However, in present-day Japan, there are too many religious figures who have forgotten their principal occupation and are just doing such part-time jobs.

第1章　太古

はじめに神様がいた

 **❶ 神道とはどんな宗教ですか？**

　わたしは神道をやまと教と呼んでいます。"やまと"は日本の異称です。それゆえ、やまと教は「ニッポン教」といった意味になります。
　さて、やまと教（神道）とは何か？　と問われるなら、それは、
　　——日本人の宗教である——
というのが正解になりそうです。なんだか肩透かしを食わせたようですが、そうではありません。これがまじめな答えなのです。
　序章において、宗教とは人間らしい生き方を教えるものだと定義しました。ただし、民族宗教においては、その人間らしい生き方はそれぞれの民族が理想とする生き方になります。やまと教は日本人の宗教ですから、日本人が理想とする生き方を日本人に教えているのです。
　では、それはどのような生き方でしょうか？　じつは、それは漠然としています。なぜなら、「このように生きるべし」と成文法の形式では示されていないからです。それは、
　　——古き良き時代に、われわれの祖先たちが生き

CHAPTER 1　ANCIENT TIMES

First There Were the Gods

66 What sort of religion is Shintoism?

I refer to Shintoism as "Yamatoism." "Yamato" is another name for Japan, "Nippon" in Japanese. Therefore, Yamatoism has the meaning of Nippon-ism (*Nippon-kyō*).

I believe Yamatoism (Shintoism) should be defined as "the religion of the Japanese people." It may seem that I am merely trying to sidestep the issue, but that is not the case. I am answering seriously.

In the introduction, I defined religion as something which teaches how one should live as a human being. However, in the case of a folk religion, this "living as a human being" refers to the way of living that each ethnic group holds as its ideal. Yamatoism is the religion of the Japanese, therefore it teaches the Japanese the way of living that the Japanese hold to be ideal.

Now, what sort of "way of life" is being referred to? In actual fact, this is quite vague. The reason for this is that it is not expressed in the form of a written law that says "you shall live this way." Instead, it is presented as "in the good old days, our ancestors lived a beautiful way of life" and says that we our-

た美しい生き方——

　があるとして、それを理想としてわれわれも生きようではないか、というものです。その古き良き時代がいつごろであるか、それは明確に示されてはいません。いや、それが歴史的に明確に示されると、かえって困るのです。

　古き良き時代は神話的に語られます。ともかく遠い昔、わたしたちの祖先がこの日本列島で美しく生きていた——といった神話的伝承をつくって、それにもとづいて子孫であるわれわれの生き方が教えられるのです。それがやまと教です。

　したがって、やまと教にはこれといった特定の聖典・教典はありません。しかし、いちおうは『古事記』や『日本書紀』『万葉集』などを聖典扱いにします。その理由は、これらの書には古き良き時代の日本人の生き方・道が示されていると考えられるからです。

　でも、現代の学者の研究によると、『古事記』や『日本書紀』の成立は８世紀であり、そこに書かれた内容は相当に当時の政治事情が反映しています。したがって、とてもとても古き良き時代からの伝承とは言えません。８世紀の時代の人々の「創作」と考えるべきでしょう。しかし、それは現代人だから言えることで、昔の人々は、『古事記』や『日本書紀』『万葉集』に、古き良き時代の純粋な日本人の生き方が表明されていると考えていたのです。

　さて、話を元に戻して、わたしは「やまと教は日本人の宗教である」と言いましたが、これは、日本人でなければやまと教の信者になれないことを意味します。外国人はやまと教の信者になれないのです。

selves should take that as our ideal and try to live that way, too. Just when that ideal period was is not clearly indicated. If that were made historically clear-cut, things would become troublesome.

The "good old days" can be treated as mythical. At any rate, in the distant past, our ancestors lived in a beautiful way on the Japanese Islands. Our way of life as descendants is taught to us based on this mythical tradition. This is how Yamatoism works.

Therefore, there are no specific scriptures or sacred writings in Yamatoism. However, after a fashion, the *Kojiki* (Record of Ancient Matters), *Nihon Shoki* (Chronicle of Japan) and the *Man'yōshū* are treated as sacred texts. The reason is that these works are thought to show "the way of life" or "the path" of the Japanese of the good old days.

According to the research of scholars in our own day, however, the *Kojiki* and *Nihon Shoki* came into existence in the 8th century, and their contents reflect the political affairs of that day considerably. Consequently, one can hardly claim that they are a transmission from the wonderful days of the ancient past. One should probably think of them as "creative works" of people of the 8th century. That, however, is how people today see them. People in the past considered the *Kojiki*, *Nihon Shoki* and *Man'yōshū* to be expressions of the genuine way of life of the Japanese of the good old days.

As I have said, Yamatoism is the religion of the Japanese, and that means that only Japanese can become believers in Yamatoism. Non-Japanese cannot become believers.

と同時に、逆に日本人であれば、すべての人がやまと教の信者にされてしまいます。そのいい例が靖国神社です。靖国神社は、明治維新とそれ以後の戦争における戦死者の霊を合祀した神社ですが、そこにはすべての日本人の戦死者の霊が祀られています。かりに遺族が、「戦死したわたしの夫はクリスチャンだから神社に祀らないでほしい」と言っても、神社のほうでは勝手に祀ってしまうのです。

　その結果、おもしろいことに日本の宗教人口は2億人を超えます。日本の総人口の1.5倍を超える信者がいるわけです。宗教人口とは、文部科学省が各教団からの報告を集計したものです。だいたいどの教団も実数に相当の水増しした信者数を報告しますが、神社本庁からは1億人に近い信者数の報告がなされます。神社本庁にすれば、日本人は全員が神道（やまと教）の信者だと思っているからそうなるのです。

　ともかくやまと教は、日本人しか信者になれず、日本人であれば全員が信者にされてしまうといった、そういう民族宗教です。

 ❷ では、やまと教の神はどういう神ですか？

　やまと教は多神教です。やまと教では「八百万の神」と言われているほど、数多くの神があります。
　ところが、その神の性格がすこぶる曖昧です。

24　第1章　太古

At the same time, everyone who happens to be Japanese is considered a believer. A good example of this is Yasukuni Shrine. Yasukuni is the shrine which enshrines together the spirits of the dead from the Meiji Restoration and the wars that have occurred since that time, and it enshrines the spirits of all Japanese who were killed in war. Even if a surviving member of the deceased's family says, 'My husband who was killed in the war was a Christian, so I do not wish his spirit to be enshrined in a Shintō shrine,' the shrine will still enshrine him as it pleases.

As a result, the population of Japanese who have a religion, interestingly enough, exceeds 200,000,000 people. That amounts to 1.5 times the entire population of the country. The religious population is the total of the figures reported by the various religious groups to the Ministry of Education, Culture, Sports, Science and Technology (MEXT). In general, most of the religious organizations inflate the actual numbers of their membership, and the Association of Shintō Shrines reports a membership of almost 100,000,000 believers. It happens this way because according to this association, all Japanese are believers in Shintoism (Yamatoism).

At any rate, it is the sort of folk religion in which only Japanese can become adherents, and anyone who is Japanese ends up being counted among its members.

What kind of gods does Yamatoism have?

Yamatoism is a polytheistic religion. There are so many gods that it is said there are "myriads of deities."

Nevertheless, the nature of those gods is extremely ambiguous.

『広辞苑』は、「神」を次のように解説しています。

> ①人間を超越した威力を持つ、かくれた存在。人知を以てはかることのできない能力を持ち、人類に禍福を降すと考えられる威霊。人間が畏怖し、また信仰の対象とするもの。
> ②日本の神話に登場する人格神。
> ③最高の支配者。天皇。
> ④神社などに奉祀される霊。
> ⑤人間に危害を及ぼし、怖れられているもの。㋐雷。なるかみ。㋑虎・狼・蛇など。
> ⑥キリスト教で、宇宙を創造して支配する、全知全能の絶対者。上帝。天帝。

　この解説もあまり明解ではありませんが、いちおうキリスト教でいう唯一絶対の神（⑥）と、やまと教の神（①〜⑤）とが根本的に違っていることは分かるはずです。それから、もう一つ注意しておいてほしいのは、①で神は威力（霊力。不思議な力）を持った存在とされているのに対して、④では神は霊（霊力）そのものだとされている点です。つまり、力（霊力）を持ったものが神なのか、力（霊力）そのものが神なのか、そこのところが曖昧になっているのがやまと教の神です。
　で、その点に注意しながら、わたし自身の「神」の分類をします。わたしは、やまと教の神は大きく二つに分けるべきだと思います。それは、A「霊力を持った神」とB「霊力そのものである神」です。

According to the *Kōjien* dictionary, the term *kami* is explained in the following ways.

(1) A concealed being which possesses powers that transcend [超越する] those of human beings. A power which is considered to possess abilities which cannot be grasped by human understanding and which determine the fortune or misfortune of human beings. Humans stand in awe of it, and it is the object of belief.

(2) A god with individuality [人格] who appears in Japanese myth.

(3) The greatest ruler. Emperor.

(4) A spirit enshrined by a shrine, etc.

(5) A being that causes harm to humans and is feared. (a) Lightning and thunder. (b) Tiger, wolf, snake, etc.

(6) In Christianity, the creator and ruler of the universe, and absolute being which is omniscient [全知の] and omnipotent [全能の]. God. Lord of Heaven.

This explanation is not particularly clear, but we can at least grasp the basic difference between the monotheistic god of Christianity (6) and the gods of Yamatoism (1–5). There is one other significant point, and that is the difference between (1), in which a *kami* is a being which possesses a mysterious, supernatural power, and (4), in which a *kami* is a spirit or supernatural power in itself. In other words, in Yamatoism it is unclear whether the *kami* (god or deity) is the being that possesses the miraculous, mysterious power or that miraculous, mysterious power itself.

Keeping that point in mind, I will offer my own classification of *kami*. I believe that the *kami* of Yamatoism should be broadly divided into two categories. Category A is "gods who possess supernatural power" and Category B is "gods who are supernatural powers."

A「霊力を持った神」は、これまた2種に分類できます。A1「固有名詞で呼ばれる神」とA2「普通名詞で呼ばれる神」です。

　A1「固有名詞で呼ばれる神」は、だいたいにおいて大きな神社に祀られている神です。イザナギノミコト（伊邪那岐命）、イザナミノミコト（伊邪那美命）、アマテラスオオミカミ（天照大神）、スサノオノミコト（素戔嗚尊）、オオクニヌシノミコト（大国主命）などがその代表です。

　また、死後に神として祀られた人もいます。平安前期の菅原道真（845-903）は、死後にさまざまな怪異が現れたため、御霊として北野天満宮に祀られて、天満天神と呼ばれるようになりました。これも「固有名詞で呼ばれる神」です。そういえば、豊臣秀吉（1537-98）は死んで豊国大明神となり、徳川家康（1542-1616）は東照大権現となって、それぞれ神社に祀られています。これらもやはり「固有名詞で呼ばれる神」です。

　次にA2「普通名詞で呼ばれる神」は、われわれの身近にいる神です。たとえば荒神がそれです。これは竈の神です。あるいは、道路の悪霊を防いで旅行者を守護してくれる道祖神もそうです。

　それから、読者はびっくりされるかもしれませんが、疫病を流行させる神である厄病神や、人を貧乏にさせると信じられている神である貧乏神も、これまた「普通名詞で呼ばれる神」です。もちろん、反対に福を授けてくれる福の神だって、「普通名詞で呼ばれる神」

道祖神

Category A, "gods who possess supernatural powers," can be subdivided into A1, "gods called by proper names," and A2, "gods called by common names."

"Gods called by proper names" (A1) are by and large enshrined in large shrines. Representative of this type are Izanagi no Mikoto, Izanami no Mikoto, Amaterasu Ōmikami, Susanoo no Mikoto and Ōkuninushi no Mikoto.

There are also humans who are worshipped as gods after their death. In the early Heian period, after the death of Sugawara no Michizane (845–903), because a number of unnatural events occurred, his vengeful spirit was worshipped at Kitano Tenmangū, and he came to be referred to as Tenman Tenjin. This is a case of a deity being referred to with a proper name. Similarly, Toyotomi Hideyoshi (1537–1598) died and became Hōkoku Daimyōjin, while Tokugawa Ieyasu (1542–1616) became Tōshō Daigongen, and both were worshipped in their respective shrines. That is exactly what we mean by referring to them with proper names.

"Gods called by common names" (A2) are gods that are close and familiar to us. One example is *kōjin*, a folk deity who supervises the kitchen fire, and is considered the deity of the kitchen stove. And then there is *dōsojin*, the gods who protect travelers along the roads from evil spirits.

It may come as a surprise to the reader, but there is also a *yakubyōgami*, a god who causes epidemics to spread, and *binbōgami*, a god who is believed to reduce people to poverty. These are deities called by common names. Of course, the gods who bring good fortune, *fuku no kami*, also belong to this group. Representative of the gods who are bringers of good luck are

の一つです。福の神の代表は七福神です。

　ここで注意しておいてほしいのは、やまと教の神は必ずしもプラスの評価を受ける存在とは限りません。プラスの方向であれマイナスの方向であれ、平均値から遠ざかっているものをやまと教では神と見ているのです。だから現代の日本人だって、野球やゴルフのずば抜けてうまい人を、「彼は野球の神様だ」「ゴルフの神様だ」と言って、神様扱いにします。一芸に秀でた者が神とされるのです。その秀で方はマイナスの方向でもかまいません。だから「泥棒の神様」だっているのです。

　ともあれ、「固有名詞で呼ばれる神」にしろ「普通名詞で呼ばれる神」にしろ、これらの神は霊力（不思議な力）を持った神です。貧乏神は人を貧乏にさせる力を持っており、福の神は人を幸福にさせる力を持っています。

　このような神のほかに、やまと教では霊力そのものも神と見ます。これがBです。ここのところがやまと教の一大特色といってよいでしょう。

　では、そのような神とは何かといえば、やまと教ではそれを、

　　——気（"き"あるいは"け"と発音されます）——

と呼びます。しかし、それがいったいどういうものであるか、なかなか説明がむずかしいのです。

　まず、この「気」はわれわれの目には見えません。目には見えないけれども、その場に漂っており、その場にいる者を支配しています。人々はその「気」の存在を感じ取るのです。それを感じ取ることのできない鈍感な人は軽蔑され、場合によっては除け者にされます。このような「気」は、日本語では"空気"と言ったり、"雰囲気"と言ったりしま

the *shichifukujin*, the seven deities of good fortune.

I would like to call your attention to the fact that the gods of Yamatoism are not always beings who are recognized as beneficial. Whether it possesses harmful or beneficial aspects, anything that is far from average is seen by Yamatoism as a *kami*. Therefore, even present-day Japanese may refer to a skillful athlete who stands head and shoulders above other competitors as the "god of baseball" (or "patron saint of baseball") or the "god of golf." Anyone who excels in a skill is made into a god. What the person excels in may also be something negative. That is why there is such a thing as a "god of thieves."

In any case, whether it is a god called by a proper name or by a common name, each is a god which possesses some supernatural power. The god of poverty has the power to make people poor. The god of fortune has the power to bring good fortune to people.

In addition to these gods, Yamatoism also sees such supernatural power itself as a *kami*. This is Category B, and it may be the single most distinguishing feature of Yamatoism.

What is this kind of deity? In Yamatoism, it is called *ki* (気, mood, frame of mind, feeling, atmosphere), and the character can also be read as *ke*.

When it comes to explaining it, however, the going gets rough. First of all, *ki* is not something that can be seen. It is not visible to the eye, but instead floats in the air of a place, and it controls those who are in that place. The people there are aware of the existence of that particular atmosphere. A person who is insensitive and cannot grasp the feeling in the air is held in low regard and in some cases is excluded. This kind of *ki* is called in Japanese *kūki* (atmosphere or spirit) and also *fun'iki*

す。たとえば会議などで、自分は反対意見であったが、「あの場の空気では、賛成せざるを得なかった」というようなことを言いますが、それは会議の場を支配している神（気）がいることを日本人は認めているからです。

その神（気）を無視する人が「空気の読めない人」と呼ばれます。

一方、この「気」はわれわれの内部にもあります。それは生命力と言ってもよいものですが、たんなる生命力ではなしに、生命を根源的に支えている力であって、それを日本語では「気力」と呼びます。そして、この内部にある「気力」が外部にある「気」と共鳴し共振したとき、「気力が充実」し「元気になる」のです。

やまと教では、このような「気」が宇宙に充満していると考えられています。その「気」を無視することなく、常に「気遣い」ながら、「気」とともに生きていこうというのがやまと教の教義だといえます。

 **❸ 日本の神道（やまと教）はアニミズムだと言う学者がいますが、いま言われたことはそうなんですか？**

人間ばかりではなしに、動物、植物や自然物、それに自然現象にまで霊魂（ラテン語で"アニマ"といいます）が宿っているというのがアニミズムです。これはイギリスの人類学者のE・B・タイラー（1832–1917）が提唱した学説です。タイラーの学説は大きな影響を及ぼしましたが、彼はまた多神教

(atmosphere or ambience). For example, in a meeting a person holding an opposing opinion might say, 'Given the atmosphere at the meeting, I had no choice but to agree.' This is because Japanese recognize that they are controlled by the *kami* or *ki*, of the meeting location.

A person who disregards that *kami* or *ki* is referred to as being "a person who cannot read, grasp, or intuit a situation."

This *ki* is also inside us. One could call it *animus* or "the power to stay alive," but it is not only that. It is the vital force or power which fundamentally supports life, which in Japanese is called *kiryoku*, or willpower. When this internal "willpower" empathizes or resonates with the external *ki*, then one becomes "full of vitality" and "spirited."

In Yamatoism, it is thought that this sort of *ki* fills the universe. One can say that it is a doctrine of Yamatoism that one should not disregard *ki*, but instead should keep it constantly in mind and live together with it.

 Some scholars say that Japanese Shintō (Yamatoism) is animistic, but is that what was just explained?

Animism is a term that means that there is a "soul" or "spirit" (called *animus* in Latin) dwelling not only in human beings, but also in animals, plants, natural physical objects and even natural phenomena. Animism is a theory put forth by the British anthropologist Edward B. Tylor (1832–1917). Tylor's theory was highly influential, but it was also vigorously criticized, due

CHAPTER 1   ANCIENT TIMES   33

から一神教へと宗教が発展するという進化主義的な態度をとったため、大きな批判も受けました。今日では、アニミズムは農耕民族のあいだに見られる文化であり、牧畜民族のあいだでは最初の段階から人格神的なものを崇拝していたとされています。

ところで、やまと教は農耕民族である日本人の民族宗教ですから、たしかにアニミズムの傾向があります。でも、それじゃあ、やまと教でいう「気」が「霊魂（アニマ）」と同じかといえば、少し違っています。アニミズムの場合、霊魂はすべての物の中に内在しています。

しかしやまと教では、「気」は生命力（あるいは気力）としてすべての物に内在していると同時に、それを離れて、その外にも、その場に漂って存在しているのです。この内在している「気」と外側にある「気」が共鳴・共振したとき、その物が元気になるのです。共鳴・共振しなければ、元気がなくなります。

どうすれば「気」と共鳴・共振できるのですか？

それはお祭りです。神様を祭ればよいのです。
神様の祭り方は、神様によってさまざまです。
まず「固有名詞で呼ばれる神」の祭り方ですが、これは賓客をお迎えする要領で祭ります。
「固有名詞で呼ばれる神」は、大きな神社に祀られています。（"まつる"という漢字には"祭"と"祀"がありますが、本書ではあまり区別しないで使います）。現代人は、神社に神が常においでになるかの

to the evolutionist view that religion develops from polytheism to monotheism. At present, it is held that animism is the culture seen among agricultural people, while it is held that among pastoral people, from the first stage individual deities are worshiped.

Yamatoism is the folk religion of the Japanese, who are an agricultural people, so there is certainly a tendency toward animism among them. If that were the case, *ki* would be the same as *reikon* (*anima*, soul or spirit), but that does not seem to be the case. In animism, *reikon* resides in everything.

However, in Yamatoism, *ki*, as a power to live or as willpower, resides in all things, while at the same time it separates from all things, and floats about, outside of those things. When the *ki* that resides inside empathizes and resonates with the *ki* floating about the place, the entity becomes energetic. If they do not resonate or vibrate in unison, they lose energy.

66 What can you do so that you resonate or vibrate in sympathy with *ki*?

The answer is festivals. Worship the gods.

The way you worship varies according to the god itself.

First, in the worship of the "gods called by a proper name," the main point is to play host to the god as an honored guest.

"A god called by a proper name" is worshipped at a large shrine. (The Chinese character for *matsuru* can be either 祭 or 祀 but in this book I do not make a distinction between the two.) People today think that the *kami* always resides inside the

ように思っていますが、教理的にはそうではありません。祭礼を行うたびごとに、神官が神をお招きし、そして祭礼が終わると神にお帰りいただきます。神社というのは、神が降臨される場であり、迎えた神をお祭りする場なのです。

　そして、降臨された神を神官は鄭重に持て成します。そうすると神は、たとえば稲のうちに内在している「気」に働きかけて、豊作をもたらしてくれるのです。海の「気」と共鳴・共振すれば大漁になるのです。

　これが「固有名詞で呼ばれる神」の祭り方です。

　次に「普通名詞で呼ばれる神」の祭り方ですが、こちらのほうは基本的にさまざまな品物を差しあげ、またさんざんに煽てあげるのです。もともと日本語の"祭る"は、"奉る・献る"（差しあげる・たてまつる）と同義の言葉です。

　神様はわれわれ人間と同じように、贈り物や煽てに弱いのです。ただ、「固有名詞で呼ばれる神」は賓客を迎えたときのように持て成し、「普通名詞で呼ばれる神」には友だちのように付き合えばよいのです。

　では、「霊力そのものである神」つまり「気」とはどのように付き合えば良いのでしょうか？　この神はわざわざお招きする必要はありません。目には見えないけれども、いつもその場に漂っているからです。

　しかしわたしたちは、ついついこの「気」の存在を忘れてしまいます。あまりにもまじめに仕事をしていると、周囲の人々の気持ちに気付かず、雰囲気

shrine, but from the point of view of traditional doctrine that is not true. Each time a festival is held, a Shintō priest invites the deity, and when the festival ends, the priest sends the deity off. The shrine is the place to which the deity descends, a place where a festival is held for the welcomed deity.

The priest respectfully shows hospitality to the *kami* which has descended. Then, the *kami* exerts influence, for example on the *ki* that resides within rice plants and brings about a good harvest. If the *kami* resonates and vibrates in sympathy with the *ki* of the sea, then that will produce a large catch for fishermen.

This is the proper way of worshipping "gods called by a proper name."

Next we will look at how to worship "gods called by common names." Basically this involves offering a variety of goods and flattering the deity endlessly. In the beginning, the Japanese word *matsuru* (deify or revere) had the same meaning as "give" or "present."

The gods are as easily swayed by presents as human beings are. A "god called by a proper name" should be entertained like an honored guest, while a "god called by a common name" should be associated with like a friend.

How should we relate with *ki*, a deity that is a supernatural power in and of itself? It is not necessary to go to the trouble of purposely inviting this god. That is because you cannot see it, but it is always floating around a particular place.

However, we inadvertently forget about the presence of this form of *ki*. When we work too seriously, we fail to notice the feelings of the people around us, and being unable to grasp the

やその場の空気を読むことができずに、自分一人が突っ張ってしまいます。そうすると知らず知らずのうちに仲間を傷つけ、あげくは自分も傷つくのです。

では、そういう状態になったらどうすればよいかといえば、この場合もお祭りをやればよいのです。しかし、「気」（霊力そのものである神）は絶えずわたしたちの身近にいるのですから、お祭りをやるといっても、わざわざ神様をお招きして饗応（きょうおう）する必要はありません。

わたしたちが「気付け」ばいいのです。また大掛かりな持て成しをするのではなく（そうしたっていっこうにかまいませんが）、仲間たちで集まってちょっとした宴会をやればいいのです。わたしたちのほうで「気」に「気付け」ば、「気」のほうは喜んでわたしたちに同調してくれます。そうすると「元気」が回復できます。

つまり、やまと教においては、お祭りが大事です。お祭りというのは、神様を招き、神様と一緒にみんなで浮かれ騒ぎます。そうすると人間は神様と「気が合」い、また人間同士でも「気が合」い、人間と万物の「気が合」い、物事はうまくいくのです。

Q❺ 「穢（けがれ）」とは何ですか？ また、「禊（みそぎ）」と「祓（はらえ）」についても説明してください。

「気」は、前にも言いましたが"き"とも"け"とも発音されます。そして、われわれがこの「気」の存在を忘れていると、われわれの内部にある生命

atmosphere of the occasion, we act one-sidedly. When that happens, without our being aware of it, we hurt our companions and ultimately hurt ourselves.

What we should do, if we find ourselves in such a situation, is to hold a festival. However, *ki* (a god that itself is a supernatural power) is constantly around us, so even though we talk about "having a festival," it is not necessary to purposely invite the god and give it a feast.

We should simply take notice of that *ki*. We do not need to offer elaborate hospitality (although we can do so if we want to), 手のこんだ
but we can simply gather our companions together and have a small party. If we just take notice of this *ki*, then it will happily harmonize with us. And when that happens, vitality will be restored.

In other words, within Yamatoism, festivals are important. In a festival, people invite the god and make merry with that god. By doing so, humans get along well with the god, human beings get along with one another, humans get along with all things under the sun and everything goes smoothly.

66 What is "impurity"? And please explain the meaning of purification and exorcism.

As we have seen, the character 気 can be read as *ki* or as *ke*. When we forget the existence of this *ki*, the vitality that is within us (which is one form of *ki*) ceases to resonate with the greater

力（それも「気」の一形態です）が外部にある大きな「気」と共鳴・共振できなくなり、「気が沈」みます。そのような状態が、

　——けがれ（気離れ）——

です。われわれが外部にある大きな「気」から離れてしまったのですね。

　じつは、この「けがれ」を「気枯れ」だと説明する学者もいます。しかし、"枯れる"も"離る"も同源の言葉ですから、わたしは"気離れ"のほうがいいと思います。

「気から離れ」て内部の生命力が不活性の状態になったのが「穢」です。

　なお、「穢」といえば、現代人は「汚いこと」「汚れた状態」を考えますが、やまと教の本来の意味は「気」が低下した状態です。

　では、こういう状態になると、われわれはどうすればいいでしょうか？　前の質問では、「気」と共鳴・共振するためには祭りをする必要があると答えましたが、ここで一つ注意すべきことがあります。それは、外部にある大きな「気」が異常になっているときです。天変地異が起きたり、身近な人が病気になったり死んだりした場合です。そういうときには浮かれたり騒いではいけません。わたしたちは、じっと身を、

　——慎む——

のです。そして、この「慎み」に入るべき状態になることが「罪」です。やまと教でいう「罪」は、仏教やキリスト教の「罪」と根本的に違っています。また、法律上の犯罪とも違っています。

ki that is outside us, and as a result we become "stagnant."

This state is called *kegare*, impurity. It means that we have separated from the great "spirit" that occupies the external world.

As it happens, there are scholars who explain *kegare* as a "withering of the spirit." However, regardless of the origin of the word, I believe that the appropriate understanding is "growing distant from the spirit."

The state in which one becomes separated from the spirit outside oneself, leaving the internal vital force inactive, is called *kegare*, impurity or defilement.

When modern people hear this word, they tend to think of something that is "dirty" or "a state of uncleanliness," but its original meaning in Yamatoism is a state in which spirit has decreased.

In such a situation, what are we to do? In the previous question, the answer was that it was necessary to hold a festival in order to resonate and sympathize with "spirit," but there is another point worth noting. It is when the great "spirit" in the outside world is abnormal. This includes times when a natural disaster occurs or when someone close to us becomes ill or dies. At such times, one should not make merry.

We should behave discreetly at such times. Coming into a state such as this is *tsumi*, or sin. What Yamatoism calls "sin" is fundamentally different from sin in Buddhism and Christianity. It is also different from being guilty of a crime.

さて、そこで、このような「罪」や「穢」から身を清める手段として、
　——「禊（みそぎ）」と「祓（はらえ）」——
があります。しかし、困ったことに「禊」と「祓」がどう違うか、統一した解釈がありません。わたしたちは両者を区別しないでおきます。

「禊」と「祓」の方法は、海や川に入ったり、滝に打たれたりする、水による方法があります。また、火祭りの火の粉を浴びる火による方法もあり、塩をまく方法もあります。大相撲の土俵に塩をまくのも、あれは「禊」と「祓」なのです。

Q6 福の神と貧乏神について教えてください。

それに答える前に、やまと教における神様との付き合い方をお話ししておきます。

神様との付き合い方は、基本的には神様をお招きして饗応することです。「固有名詞で呼ばれる神」に対しては、賓客を正式に招待するようにします。「普通名詞で呼ばれる神」に対しては、あまり格式張らずに友だちを呼んだときのように持て成せばよいのです。しかし、いずれにしても、神様にお越しいただいて、心をこめて神様を持て成すのです。それが基本姿勢です。

そうだとすると、神様にお願いごとをするのはおかしいと思いませんか。お願いごと、頼みごとをするために人を招待すれば、たいていの人は怒りますよね。ましてや神様に来ていただいて、それに願いごとをすべきではありません。

Now then, the way to purify the self from sin (*tsumi*) and impurity (*kegare*) is purification (*misogi*) and exorcism (*harae*). However, awkwardly enough, there is no standardized interpretation of how purification and exorcism differ. Let us try not to distinguish between the two.

Among methods of purification and exorcism, some involve water, such as entering a sea or a river or standing under a waterfall. Other methods include the use of fire—at a fire festival or being covered with the sparks of fire—and the scattering of salt. The scattering of salt in the ring (*dohyō*) of professional sumō is purification and exorcism.

❝ Please explain about the "god of fortune" and the "god of poverty."

Before answering the question, let me say something about how Yamatoism says you should relate with the gods.

Relationships with the gods are basically a case of inviting them and offering them a feast. For a "god called by a proper name" that means formally inviting it as an the honored guest. For a "god called by a common name" it is like the hospitality you offer when you informally invite a friend to do something. However, in either case, you have the god come and you make it welcome. That is the fundamental attitude.

That being the case, does it not seem strange if you make a request of the god? If you invite someone for the purpose of making a request or asking a favor, that person would almost invariably be angry. Still more, if you have invited a god, you certainly ought not ask a favor of it.

わたしは、神様に願いごとをすることを「請求書の祈り」と呼んでいます。それは良くない祈りです。神様に祈りを捧げるのは、感謝のための祈りです。その感謝のための祈りを、わたしは「領収書の祈り」と命名しました。
　じつは、やまと教の祈りは、基本的には「領収書の祈り」です。現代日本人は、神様にお願いごとをする──請求書の祈り──のがやまと教だと思っている人が多いのですが、それはやまと教に対する現代人の無知のなせることです。やまと教の本質は、感謝の心──領収書の祈り──でもって神様に接することにあります。
　したがって、福の神を招いて、これにお願いごとをしようなどといったさもしい根性はいけません。そんな根性で福の神に接すると、福の神が疫病神に変身する可能性があります。逆に貧乏神を忌避することもよくない。貧乏神を忌避すればするほど、ますます貧乏神は祟ります。
　そこで、福の神に感謝のこころで接すると同時に、貧乏神にも感謝のこころで接します。そうすると貧乏神はあなたに祟りません。それがやまと教の考え方です。
　そもそも福の神と貧乏神は一枚のコインの裏と表の関係です。あるいは、いつも一緒に行動する姉妹神です。貧乏神を毛嫌いせずに仲良くしていると、福の神も喜んでくれます。それは、病気になっても、病気と仲良く暮らすという考え方に通じます。そのような生き方を、やまと教はわれわれに教えてくれているのです。

I call asking a god for a favor "an invoice prayer." This is not a good kind of prayer. Offering up a prayer to a god should be a prayer of gratitude. I call this type of prayer of gratefulness "a receipt prayer."

In reality the prayers of Yamatoism are fundamentally "receipt prayers." A large percentage of Japanese today believe that asking the gods for something—an "invoice prayer"—is Yamatoism, but this just shows how ignorant they are regarding Yamatoism. The true essence of Yamatoism is to deal with the gods with an attitude of gratitude—through "receipt prayers."

Consequently, one should not be of such a base spirit that one invites a god of fortune and then asks a favor of it. If you deal with the god of good fortune with such a spirit, it is possible that the god of fortune will turn into a god of epidemics. Conversely, it is not wise to avoid a god of poverty. The more you shun the god of poverty, the more punishment he will inflict.

Therefore, at the same time one attends to the god of fortune with gratitude, one should also attend to the god of poverty with gratitude. That is the proper way of thinking according to Yamatoism.

To begin with, the god of fortune and the god of poverty are related to one another like two sides of the same coin. Sometimes the two are companion gods who act together. If you do not take an aversion to the god of poverty but stay on friendly terms with it, the god of fortune will also be pleased. The same holds true for living peacefully with an illness when you get sick. Yamatoism teaches us this way of living.

Q❼ 七福神というのは福の神ですね。

　代表的な福徳の神様を7人集めて「七福神」として信仰するようになったのは、室町時代のころからとされています。しかし、誰と誰をもって七福神とするかに関しては諸説紛々。最もポピュラーなのは次の7人です。

1　大黒天……もとはインドのヒンドゥー教の神様で、インド名はマハーカーラ。日本に来て大黒天は、"だいこく"が"大国"に通じるところから、オオクニヌシノカミ（大国主神）と同一視されるようになりました。それゆえこの神は、ヒンドゥー教とやまと教の混血の神です。

2　恵比須……"夷""恵比寿"とも表記されます。純粋に日本の神様で、本来は漁民の神。のちに海運守護の神となり、また商売繁昌の神様になりました。

3　毘沙門天……別名を多聞天といい、インド出身の仏教の守護神。財宝と福徳のほか、子宝も授けてくれます。

4　弁財天……俗に"弁天さま"と呼ばれます。ヒンドゥー教の河川神であるサラスヴァティーが仏教にとり入れられたもので、本来は"弁才天"といって音楽、弁

弁財天

❝ The Seven Deities of Good Fortune are included among the gods of fortune, right?

Belief in the seven representative gods of happiness and prosperity, known as the "Seven Gods of Good Fortune," is said to have sprung up sometime around the Muromachi period. However, there are conflicting opinions regarding exactly which gods are included in the group. The following seven are the most popular.

(1) Daikokuten——Originally a Hindu god in India, the Indian name is Mahakala. Upon reaching Japan, his name Daikoku was homophonous with an alternate reading of the god Ōkuni-nushi-no-kami, so they were seen as identical. Therefore, this god is of mixed background, Hinduism and Yamatoism.

(2) Ebisu——There are two different ways to write this name in characters. A purely Japanese deity, originally the god of fishing people. Eventually, Ebisu became the guardian deity of sea transportation as well as the god of business.

(3) Bishamonten——Also known as Tamonten, this god of Indian descent is the guardian deity of Buddhism. In addition to wealth and good fortune, this god also confers children on couples.

(4) Benzaiten——Popularly called "Benten-sama." The river god of Hinduism, Sarasvati was introduced into Buddhism. Originally 弁才天 (Benzaiten), this was a female deity of music, eloquence and wisdom. Later, the name was written

舌、知恵の女神でした。ところが後世になると、"弁財天"と表記されて金運の女神になりました。

5 福禄寿……中国の民間信仰（道教）の神で、南極星の化身とされています。精神的幸福と物質的な富、長寿をかなえてくれるという、三拍子そろった神様です。

福禄寿

6 寿老人……福禄寿の別名とされています。とくに長寿を授けてくれる神です。

7 布袋……この人は歴史的人物で、中国・後梁時代の禅僧でした。その恬淡とした生き方から福の神とされたのです。

なお、寿老人が福禄寿の異名同体の神様であるところから、これをはぶいて吉祥天を七福神に加えることもあります。吉祥天はヒンドゥー教の女神で、毘沙門天の妃になります。幸福と知恵を授けてくれる神様です。

弁財天 (Benzaiten) and she became the female deity of wealth.

(5) Fukurokuju——A deity from Daoism, Chinese folk religion, held to be an incarnation of the south pole star. An all-round deity who is believed to grant spiritual happiness, material wealth and long life.

(6) Jurōjin——Considered another name for Fukurokuju. Especially confers long life.

(7) Hotei——A historical figure from China, Ch'an (Zen) priest of the Late Lian period. Due to his unselfish way of life, he became a god of fortune.

Further, Jurōjin and Fukurokuju are considered different names for the same deity, so sometimes Jurōjin is left out and replaced by Kichijōten in the Seven Deities. Kichijōten is a female deity from Hinduism and a consort (配偶者) of Bishamonten. She is a deity who grants happiness and prosperity as well as wisdom.

第 2 章　飛鳥―奈良時代

仏教が日本にやって来た

Q❶　インドの宗教が日本に入って来て、日本の宗教とのあいだに摩擦はなかったのですか？

　仏教はなるほどインドに発祥した宗教です。仏教の開祖である釈迦(しゃか)（前566–前486。ただし異説もあります）はインド人です。
　もっとも、仏教には、小乗仏教(しょうじょう)と大乗仏教(だいじょう)という、まったく違った2種があります。両者の違いはユダヤ教とキリスト教ほど違っています。小乗仏教がユダヤ教的で、大乗仏教はキリスト教的です。

　小乗仏教においては、釈迦は人間として扱われます。釈迦国の太子として生まれた一人の人間が29歳で出家し、6年間の修行ののち35歳で悟りを開いてブッダ（仏陀）となった。"ブッダ"というサンスクリット語は、「（宇宙の真理に）目覚めた人」を意味します。その仏陀の教えが仏教です。

　ところが、大乗仏教においては、釈迦は人間ではなく、はじめから仏であります。すなわち、時間と空間を超越した宇宙そのものである仏（これを宇宙仏と呼べばよいでしょう）の真理を説くために、宇

CHAPTER 2   ASUKA–NARA PERIOD

Buddhism Arrives in Japan

> **When Indian Buddhism came to Japan, was there conflict with Japanese religion?**

Buddhism of course originated in India. Its founder, Shakyamuni (BCE 566–486, there are other theories), was Indian.

There are two completely different varieties of Buddhism called Hinayana and Mahayana. The difference between the two is as large as the difference between Judaism and Christianity. Hinayana resembles Judaism, while Mahayana resembles Christianity.

Within Hinayana Buddhism, Shakyamuni is treated as a human being. This individual human being was born a prince of the Sakya clan, became a monk at the age of 29, and after six years of practicing austerities, at the age of 35 he achieved enlightenment and became the Buddha. The Sanskrit word "Buddha" means "the one who has awakened (to the truth of the universe)." The teachings of Buddha are Buddhism.

In Mahayana Buddhism, however, Shakyamuni is not a human being but rather a buddha from the very beginning. In other words, in order to teach the truth of the Buddha (which we may call the cosmic Buddha), which is the cosmos itself that

宙仏が人間の姿をとって降臨されたのが釈迦である——と見ているのです。ですから、この考え方はキリスト教と同じです。キリスト教では、宇宙を創造された神が、宇宙の真理を啓示するために神の子であるイエスを人間世界に遣わしたとしています。(図参照)

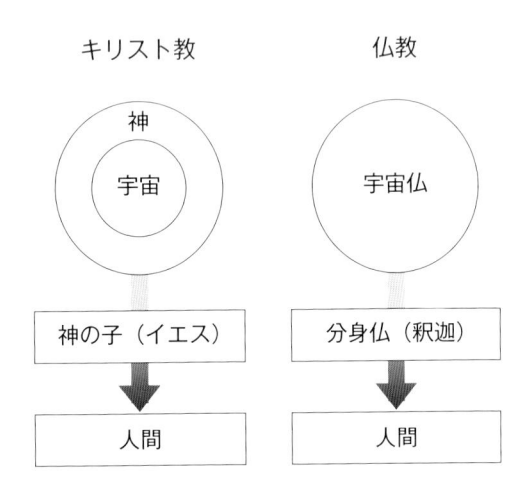

```
      キリスト教              仏教

       ┌─神─┐              ┌────┐
       │宇宙│              │宇宙仏│
       └────┘              └────┘
          ↓                    ↓
    ┌──────────┐       ┌──────────┐
    │神の子(イエス)│     │分身仏(釈迦)│
    └──────────┘       └──────────┘
          ↓                    ↓
       ┌────┐              ┌────┐
       │人間│              │人間│
       └────┘              └────┘
```

　そして、日本に伝来した仏教は、この大乗仏教です。大乗仏教はインドから中央アジアを経由して中国に伝わり、中国から朝鮮半島を経て日本に伝わって来ました。日本に伝来したのは538年（一説によると552年）です。百済の聖明王が日本の皇室に、一体の仏像と若干の仏具や経典を献じて来たのが「仏教の公伝」とされています。

■■■

　さて、伝来した仏教を受容すべきか否か、欽明天皇は臣下たちに諮問しました。
　その諮問に対する答申は二つに分かれます。一つ

transcends time and space, this cosmic Buddha descended to earth in human form as Shakyamuni. Therefore, the Mahayana way of thinking is the same as that of Christianity. In Christianity, the deity who created the universe sent his son Jesus to the world of humanity in order to manifest the truth of the universe. (See illustration)

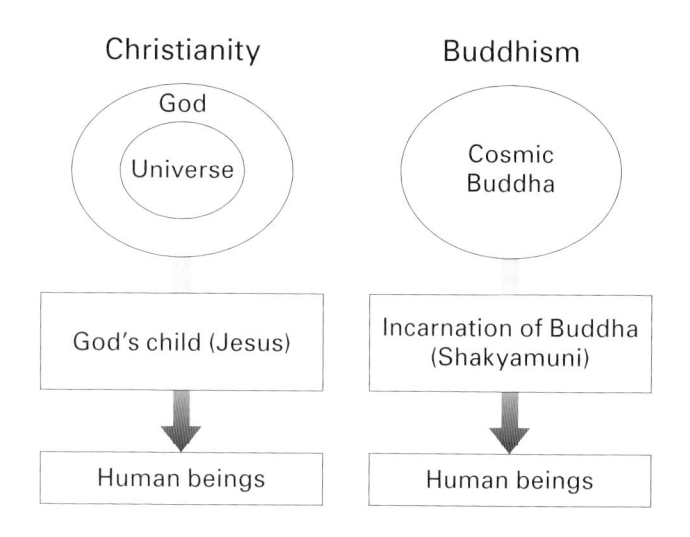

```
      Christianity              Buddhism
         God                    
       Universe              Cosmic Buddha

   God's child (Jesus)    Incarnation of Buddha
                              (Shakyamuni)
           ↓                       ↓
      Human beings            Human beings
```

The form of Buddhism which was introduced to Japan was Mahayana. This was transmitted from India via Central Asia to China, and then by way of the Korean peninsula to Japan. Buddhism was introduced into Japan in 538 (some say 552). The introduction of Buddhism is held to be when Syongmyong of Paekche sent to Japan's imperial house an image of Shakyamuni, a number of articles for a Buddhist altar and Buddhist sutras.

Emperor Kinmei consulted with his retainers as to whether the imported Buddhism should be accepted or not.

Reponses to this consultation were divided into two camps.

は、蘇我稲目からの答申で「崇仏論」です。もう一つは、物部尾輿と中臣鎌子からの「排仏論」の答申でした。

「崇仏論」は、中国や朝鮮半島の諸国が仏教を採用している、そういう国際情勢に鑑みて、わが国も仏教を受け容れるべきだ、というものです。「排仏論」は、仏教という外国の神様を受容すると、わが国固有の神々が怒るに違いないから受け容れるべきではない、という主張です。

　注意しておいてほしいのは、ここで仏教が「外国の神様」とされている点です。仏教の教義からすれば、仏と神はまったく違った存在ですから、これは誤解です。しかし、中国から朝鮮半島を経由して日本に伝来した大乗仏教では、仏は神様とそれほど違いのない存在になっています。だから、これは当たらずといえども遠からずです。半分誤解で半分正解と言うべきでしょう。

　では、相反する二つの答申に天皇はどうしたか……？　そこが日本的な解決方法で、天皇は仏像や仏具、経典を崇仏派の蘇我稲目に授けて、

「試しに拝んでみなさい」

　と言ったのです。拝んでみて効果があれば採用する、効果がなければ採用しない。そういう決定法でありました。

■■■

　ところが、その効果は逆効果でした。

　蘇我稲目が仏像礼拝を始めてしばらくすると、国に疫病の流行がありました。それで排仏派から、これは外国の神を拝んだから、わが国の神様が怒っておられるのだと抗議があります。そのため仏像は川

The response from Soga no Iname was "accept Buddhism." The response from Mononobe no Okoshi and Nakatomi no Kamako was "reject Buddhism."

The argument in favor of Buddhism, taking into account the international state of affairs in which Buddhism had been accepted by China and various countries of the Korean peninsula, concluded that Japan should also approve Buddhism. The argument against Buddhism insisted that if Japan accepted the foreign deities of Buddhism, Japan's native deities would undoubtedly be angered, so Buddhism should not be accepted.

Please note the description of Buddhism as "foreign deities." From the stance of Buddhist doctrines, buddhas (*hotoke*) and gods (*kami*) are entirely different beings, so their argument is based on misunderstanding. However, in Mahayana Buddhism which was introduced into Japan, a buddha and god are not that different. So, while they are not equivalent, they were not that much different. We should perhaps say it was a case of being half-mistaken and half-correct.

What did the emperor do with these two opposing verdicts? He took a typically Japanese method of settling the issue by conferring the Buddhist image, altar instruments and sutras on Soga no Iname, saying 'have a try at worshipping these.' If worshipping yielded results, Buddhism would be adopted. If there were no results, then it would not be adopted. That is the way the decision was made.

However, the result was counterproductive. Shortly after Soga no Iname began making offerings to the Buddhist image, an epidemic spread throughout the country. The anti-Buddhist faction argued that this was because the native deities were angry because foreign deities were being worshipped. The image of

に流して捨てられ、寺は焼かれてしまいます。結局は、最初に伝来した仏教は日本に定着しませんでした。

けれども、当時の国際情勢からすれば、日本が仏教国になるのは当然の趨勢でした。その後、584年に第2回目の仏教伝来があり、蘇我稲目の子の蘇我馬子が仏像の礼拝を始めます。しかし、このときも疫病の流行があり、最初と同じように仏像が川に流され、寺がこわされ、仏具が焼かれたりしました。

ところがこのたびは前回とちょっと様子が違って、仏教を弾圧するとますます疫病の流行がひどくなったのです。そこで、これは仏教を弾圧したたたりだということになり、蘇我馬子が私的に仏教を信仰することが許されました。このとき、私的というかたちであっても、いちおう仏教が日本に受容されたのです。

その後、585年に即位した用明天皇は、即位の翌年に病気になります。そして天皇は、その病気平癒のために仏教への帰依を表明しました。ここにおいてはっきりと仏教は日本に受容されたことになります。

Q❷ そうすると、仏教と神道（やまと教）とのあいだに、宗教戦争といったものはなかったわけですね。

信奉する宗教の教義が違い、お互いに相手の教義を異端・邪説と否定するところから起きる戦争を宗教戦争と名づけるなら、やまと教と仏教とのあいだに宗教戦争なんてものはありません。

Buddha was thrown into a river and the temple that had been built was burned to the ground. In the end, the first time Buddhism was introduced to Japan, it did not take hold.

But given the international state of affairs of that period, Japan's becoming a Buddhist country was a matter of course. In 584, Buddhism was introduced a second time, and Iname's son, Soga no Umako, enshrined a Buddhist image and worshipped it. Once again an epidemic broke out, the image was tossed into a river, the temple was destroyed and the altar fittings were burned.

But things were different on this occasion. When opponents suppressed Buddhism, the epidemic worsened. This was taken as a *divine punishment* for cracking down on Buddhism, and Soga no Umako was given permission to embrace Buddhism privately. Even though this was a private matter, this in effect meant that Buddhism was more or less accepted in Japan.

Emperor Yōmei assumed the throne in 585 but fell ill the very next year. Wishing to recover his health, the emperor declared his devotion to Buddhism and it is at this point that it can be clearly said that Buddhism was received in Japan.

> **So, does that mean that there was no religious war between Buddhism and Yamatoism?**

If by "religious war" one means conflict that occurs because of differences in the doctrine of the religion and mutual denial of the other side's doctrines as heresy, then there was no such war between Yamatoism and Buddhism.

なぜかといえば、やまと教は確たる教義を持たない宗教だからです。漠然とした、
　——われわれ日本人の生き方——
を教える民族宗教がやまと教です。しかもその解釈は人によってまちまちです。仏教は異端・邪説だから排斥せねばならないといった主張は、本来のやまと教からは出てきません。

しかし、仏教が伝来したとき、その受容を拒否する反対勢力があったではないか、と言われるかもしれません。でも、それは、日本固有の神様を拝むことが大事で、わざわざ外国から神様を導入する必要はない、といった程度の反対だったと見るべきでしょう。

仏像を川に流したり、寺院を焼いたりしたのも、あるいは、それが日本人の習俗であったとも考えられます。すなわち、やまと教の風習は、神を祭るときには祭場をつくってそこに神を降臨させます。そして祭りが終われば祭場をこわし、焼き払います。また、禊や祓のときには人形をつくってそれで身体を撫でて、災厄をこの人形に移し、そのあと人形を川に流します。このようなやまと教のやり方が、仏教や寺院に適用されたのではないかとも考えられます。そうだとすると、それを弾圧と見る必要もなくなります。

そして、結果を見てください。用明天皇は病気平癒の祈願のために仏教への帰依を表明しました。しかしこれは、用明天皇がやまと教の信者であることをやめたわけではありません。彼はやまと教の信者のまま仏教に帰依したのです。一神教の世界で、こんなことが考えられるでしょうか。イスラム教徒のままキリスト教徒になることができますか!?　やまと教だとそれが

The reason is that Yamatoism is a religion that does not possess definite doctrines. It is simply a folk religion that teaches a rather vague notion of "the Japanese way of life." Moreover, the interpretation of what that amounts to varies according to the person. There was no assertion from the original Yamatoism that Buddhism was a heretical teaching and therefore should be rejected on religious grounds.

But, you may ask, when Buddhism was introduced, was there not an opposing force that rejected its adoption? To a degree, yes, but one should probably see it more as a case of stressing worship of Japan's native deities, and saying it was unnecessary to purposely introduce gods from other countries.

As likely as not, throwing the Buddhist images into a river and burning down the temples was a Japanese folkway. That is to say, the customs of Yamatoism when worshipping a god is to construct a site for the religious celebration and have the god descend upon that site. Then when the festival is over, one destroys the site and burns it down. Similarly, in purification and exorcism, one make a figure of a human, strokes the body, transfers misfortune to this figure and then throws that figure into a river. It is possible that this process from Yamatoism was applied to Buddhism and its temples. If that is the case, then it is not necessary to view the response as a form of suppression.

And also look at how things worked out. Emperor Yōmei declared his belief in Buddhism in order to pray for recovery of his health. However, this did not mean that he ceased to be a believer in Yamatoism. He became a believer in Buddhism, while remaining a believer in Yamatoism. Is this imaginable in a world of monotheist religions? Is it conceivable that one could remain a Muslim and also be a Christian? With Yamatoism, it

できるのです。それゆえ、やまと教の場合は、宗教戦争というものはあり得ないと思います。

　と同時に、もう一つ注意すべきことがあります。それは、「仏教伝来」とか「仏教の受容」といっても、本当に仏教が伝来したのか、日本人は本当に仏教を受容したのか、という疑問です。答えは明白です。日本人は仏教を受容しなかった。日本人が受容したのは「仏教という名がついた神様」でした。そう言ったほうがよいでしょう。

　それゆえ、本物の仏教が入って来たわけではないのですから、仏教とやまと教のあいだに宗教戦争が起こるわけがありませんね。

Q❸ だとすると、日本を「仏教国」と呼ぶのはおかしいということになりますね。でも聖徳太子は立派な仏教者であったのではありませんか？

　日本を「仏教国」と呼ぶこともできますが、その場合の仏教は相当に日本化したものです。日本化したということは、やまと教化したことと同義です。やまと教化してしまった仏教（それも完璧に近いまでのやまと教化です）は、「仏教」とは言えない。そういう意味では日本は仏教国ではありません。

　仏教が日本に伝来したとき、日本人は、
「おや、われわれと違った生き方があるのだ」
と気づきました。自分たちとは違った生き方（それを教えているのが仏教です）があることが分かって、逆に「自分たちの生き方」のあることを知ることができたのです。その「自分たちの生き方」こそがやまと教です。

is possible. As a result, with Yamatoism, religious war is simply not possible.

At the same time, there is one more point to make note of. That is, when we talk about the "introduction of Buddhism" or the "acceptance of Buddhism," there is doubt as to whether Buddhism was actually introduced or accepted. The answer is clear. The Japanese did not accept Buddhism. What they did was to accept the deities included within Buddhism. That is a more accurate way of phrasing the situation.

For that reason, because true Buddhism was not introduced, no religious war between Buddhism and Yamatoism ever broke out.

> **In that case, it is strange to speak of Japan as "a Buddhist country." But then again, wasn't Prince Shōtoku a great Buddhist?**

Japan can be called "a Buddhist country," but that Buddhism was considerably Japanized. To say that it was Japanized is the same as saying that it was influenced by Yamatoism. This Yamatoism-affected Buddhism (which was virtually completely Yamatoized) cannot really be called Buddhism. In that sense, Japan is not a Buddhist country.

When Buddhism found its way into Japan, the Japanese realized, "Mmm, there's a way to live that is different from our way." Once they realized through Buddhism that there was a different way of living, on the contrary, they realized that they had their own distinct way of life. Their own "way of living" was Yamatoism.

したがって、仏教伝来の意味は、ある意味では、
——やまと教の発見——
であったと思います。その仏教によって自分たちの生き方を変えねばならぬといった意識は生じなかったようです。

もっとも、一般的にはそうなんですが、なかには仏教（仏教の生き方）を真剣に学ぼうとするごく少数の人間がいたはずです。それは例外的な人たちです。その例外的な人たちの代表が聖徳太子（574–622）です。

聖徳太子は、わが国で最初に仏教への帰依を表明した用明天皇の皇子です。用明天皇のあと、崇峻天皇を経て推古天皇が即位しますが、聖徳太子はその推古天皇の摂政皇太子となり、内政や外交に関与します。そして、多くの寺院を建立し、またみずから仏典の注釈書をつくるほどの崇仏論者でした。ただし、近年の歴史家のなかには、従来の「聖徳太子像」は相当に伝説化されたものであって、実際はそうではないと主張する人もいます。

聖徳太子

Q❹ 奈良時代といえば、東大寺の大仏が有名ですが……。

聖徳太子が摂政になる5年前（589年）、隋が中国大陸を統一しました。分裂していた中国が統一国家になったのだから、この統一国家の勢力が国外に進出して、日本にまで及ぶ可能性（日本側からすれば危険）があります。また、実際、失敗に終わったものの隋の第2代皇帝の煬帝（在位604–618）は、

Consequently, in one sense, the meaning of the introduction of Buddhism was the discovery of Yamatoism. They did not become conscious of the need to change their way of living through Buddhism.

Though this was generally the case, there must have been at least a few people who seriously attempted to draw lessons from Buddhism (i.e., a Buddhist way of living). There were exceptions. Representative of these exceptions was Prince Shōtoku (574–622).

Prince Shōtoku was the son of Emperor Yōmei, the first in Japan to declare his belief in Buddhism. After Yōmei, Emperor Sushun took the throne, followed by Empress Suiko, and Prince Shōtoku was made regent and crown prince under Suiko, directing both domestic and foreign affairs. A great proponent of Buddhism, he had many temples built and he himself wrote commentaries on Buddhist scriptures. Yet among historians of recent years there are some who claim that the traditional image of Prince Shōtoku has been mythologized to a considerable degree.

66 When you speak of the Nara period, the Great Buddha at Tōdaiji comes to mind, doesn't it?

Five years prior to Prince Shōtoku becoming regent (589), the Sui unified the Chinese mainland. Although it had once been divided, once China became a unified state its influence as a consolidated country found its way to foreign countries, possibly reaching Japan. (From the Japanese side, this meant danger.) Although they actually ended in failure, the second Sui

3度にわたって高句麗に遠征しています。

　そうすると、日本は、国の体制を斉えて隋と外交する必要があります。その国の体制を固めるために使われたのが仏教です。聖徳太子は個人的にも仏教の信奉者でしたが、当時の国際情勢からすれば、日本は形の上では仏教国にならざるを得なかったのです。
　そこで、聖徳太子の没後の2年目（624年）には、『日本書紀』の記述によりますと、
　　寺院の数……46寺
　　僧尼の数……1385人（僧816人、尼569人）
となっています。形式的には日本は立派な仏教国になったわけです。ただし、これらの寺院のほとんどは諸豪族によって建立された私寺であったことを忘れないでください。

■ ■ ■

　さて、それから100年以上ものちの752年に、聖武天皇の発願によって奈良の東大寺大仏が造営されました。この大仏は、正しくは毘盧舎那仏といいます。これはサンスクリット語の"ヴァイローチャナ・ブッダ"を音訳したもので、「輝きわたるもの」の意味です。宇宙の中心にあって四方八方に光を投げかけている太陽をイメージした仏です。つまり東大寺の大仏（毘盧舎那仏）は、「太陽の仏」であり「宇宙の仏」です。だから、巨大な仏像になっています。
　これでお分かりのように、聖武天皇は絶大なる王権の象徴として、日本の中心にあって日本全国を照らす太陽仏・宇宙仏である毘盧舎那仏を、奈良の都に安置することを考えたわけです。

大仏

emperor Yang-di (Yang-ti, reigned 604–618) sent three military expeditions against Kokuryo, in the Korean peninsula.

Given the situation, Japan found it necessary to organize the country and negotiate with the Sui. It was Buddhism that was used to solidify the structure of the government. Prince Shōtoku was privately a follower of Buddhism, but due to the international situation of the time, Japan had to become a Buddhist nation in a formal sense.

Therefore, according to the description of the *Nihon Shoki*, in 624, two years after the death of Prince Shōtoku, there were 46 Buddhist temples and 1,385 priests and nuns (816 priests and 569 nuns) in the country.

In form, Japan was a splendid Buddhist country. However, it should not be forgotten that almost all of these temples were private temples erected by the powerful clans.

■ ■ ■

A century or so passed, and in 752 the Great Buddha at Tōdaiji, which Emperor Shōmu had decreed be built, was completed. The Great Buddha is Rushana (Birushana) Buddha. This is a transliteration of the Sanskrit for Vairocana, and it means "the great light." It is a buddha with the image of the sun at the center of the universe casting light in all directions. In other words, the Great Buddha (Vairocana Buddha) at Tōdaiji is "the sun Buddha," and "the cosmic Buddha." That is why the image is enormous in size.

From this you can see that Emperor Shōmu's idea was to place, in the capital at Nara, a great image of Vairocana, the Buddha of the sun and the Buddha of the universe as the greatest symbol of royal authority. Consequently, the Great Buddha

したがって大仏は、海外に向けて国威を発揚するための王権のシンボルでありました。

Q❺ 奈良時代には道鏡という僧もいましたね。

　前にも述べたように、仏教伝来の当初に建立された寺院は、ほとんどが諸豪族によって建立された私寺でした。ところが奈良時代になると、多数の官寺が建立されます。そして官寺には、田地と封戸（労働力としての農民）が政府から与えられます。また、官寺には有力貴族からの寄進もあります。そうすると寺院経済は豊かになりますが、同時に僧侶の堕落も始まります。

　とくに僧侶が政治に関与するようになり、その結果、政治のほうも乱れてしまいました。政界に波瀾を起こした僧として有名なのが、玄昉（？-746）と道鏡（？-772）の2人です。玄昉は学問僧として入唐し、法相宗の教学を学び、時の玄宗皇帝から信任を受けたほどの高僧でした。だが、帰朝後は政治権力と結びつき、最後は失脚して左遷されます。

　同じく道鏡も、政治権力と結びついて僧の世界の最高位にまで登りつめました。そして、みずから天皇になろうとするまでの野望を起こしましたが、やはり最後は左遷されました。
　このように、奈良時代の最後は、仏教と政治権力との癒着が大きな問題になっています。

was a symbol of royal power enhancing national prestige across the seas.

🙶 Who was the Nara period monk named Dōkyō?

As mentioned previously, the temples first built following the introduction of Buddhism were almost entirely private temples built by the various powerful clans. During the Nara period, however, numbers of government-sponsored temples were built. And these government-sponsored temples were given rice fields and vassal households (farming people to serve as laborers) by the government. These government-related temples also received donations from the prominent clans. The economic conditions of these temples improved significantly but at the same time the priesthood began to decline.

The priests became involved in politics and politics also became corrupted. The two priests who are well known for causing turmoil in the government are Genbō (?-746) and Dōkyō (?-772). Genbō went to T'ang China as a scholar-priest, learned the teachings of the Fa-hsiang (Faxiang, Hossō) sect and was a high-ranking priest who gained the confidence of Emperor Xuazon. However, upon his return from abroad he became linked with political power and in the end lost power and was banished.

Similarly Dōkyō became involved in political affairs and ascended to the top position in the Buddhist priesthood. His ambitions led him to attempt to become emperor, but in the end, his influence waned and he too was banished.

In this manner, at the end of the Nara period, the close ties between Buddhism and political authority had become a major problem.

Q6 鑑真の来日について教えてください。

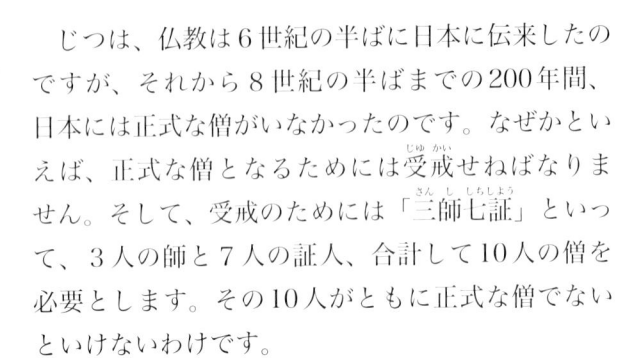

　じつは、仏教は6世紀の半ばに日本に伝来したのですが、それから8世紀の半ばまでの200年間、日本には正式な僧がいなかったのです。なぜかといえば、正式な僧となるためには受戒せねばなりません。そして、受戒のためには「三師七証」といって、3人の師と7人の証人、合計して10人の僧を必要とします。その10人がともに正式な僧でないといけないわけです。

　しかし、島国である日本では10人もの正式な僧が得られず、正式に受戒した僧はいなかったのです。ですから、前に出てきた「僧尼の数」というのは、形だけの僧尼であって正式の僧尼ではありません。

　そこでわが国は中国から授戒に必要な僧を招請しました。その招請に応えて来朝したのが唐僧の鑑真（688-763）です。

　しかし、鑑真が日本に来るには多くの困難がありました。中国側で高僧の鑑真の出国を願わぬ弟子たちの妨害があったほか、船の難破もあり、5度の失敗の末に6度目にようやく渡航がなったのです。そのあいだに鑑真は失明しています。

　だが、ともかく鑑真は授戒に必要な弟子を連れて754年に来朝しました。そして、東大寺に戒壇院を設けて授戒を行い、晩年は唐招提寺に戒律研究の道場をつくって、多くの弟子を育てました。

　この鑑真の来朝によって、わが国の仏教がようやく本物になったといえます。

鑑真

🙶 Please explain about the arrival of Ganjin.

Buddhism actually reached Japanese shores in the mid-6th century, but during the two centuries following up until the 8th century, there were no formally ordained priests in Japan. This is because in order to formally become a priest one had to be confirmed, and doing that required "three priests and seven witnesses," a total of ten priests. All ten of these had to be official priests.

However there were not ten formally recognized priests in all of the island country, so priests could not be formally ordained. Therefore, the previously mentioned figures of priests and nuns were not actually formal priests or nuns at all.

Accordingly, Japan issued a request for the necessary priests for ordination to be sent from China. The T'ang priest who responded to this request was Ganjin (688–763).

However, Ganjin encountered many obstacles in reaching Japan. From the Chinese viewpoint, he encountered resistance from his disciples who naturally did not want the venerable priest to leave the country. Then there was a shipwreck. After five unsuccessful attempts, on the sixth attempt Ganjin reached Japanese shores. In that interval, Ganjin even lost his eyesight.

Nonetheless, Ganjin reached Japan in 754, with the required number of disciple priests to perform ordinations. He established an ordination platform at Tōdaiji, carried out ordinations, and in his late years established Tōshōdaiji as a place for teaching the precepts to a large number of disciples.

With the arrival of Ganjin, true Buddhism could finally be said to have arrived in Japan.

Q❼ 儒教と道教も日本に伝来していますね。いつごろ伝来したのですか？

　儒教の日本への伝来に関しては、『日本書紀』と『古事記』が記事を載せています。それによると、応神天皇の15年に百済王の使者として阿直岐（『日本書紀』による表記。『古事記』だと阿知吉師）が日本に来ました。

　そしてこの阿直岐の推輓によって翌年、王仁（『古事記』のほうは和邇吉師）が『論語』（10巻）と『千字文』（1巻）を持って来日しました。古来、この王仁の来朝をもって、儒教の日本への伝来としています。そして、この応神天皇の16年は、朝鮮の文献によって405年と傍証されています。

　けれども、朝廷に『論語』が献上された年（405年）をもって儒教の伝来とするのは、いささか形式的にすぎるでしょう。それ以前に中国大陸や朝鮮半島からの人々の往来があるのですから、そのうちには儒教の経典に知識のある人がいて、彼らが儒教を日本人に教えていた可能性は大いにあります。

■■■

　道教というのは、一口に言えば中国人の民族宗教です。儒教と道教との関係は、わが国の皇室神道とやまと教との関係に相当します。皇室神道とは、国家権力の担い手である皇室が信奉している神道です。

　したがって、道教という宗教が、たとえば仏教や

❝ When did Confucianism and Taoism reach Japan?

An account of the arrival of Confucianism can be found in the *Nihon Shoki* and in the *Kojiki*. According to these chronicles, the Korean scholar Achiki arrived in Japan in the 15th year of the reign of Emperor Ōjin as an emissary of the king of Paekche. (He is called Achiki in the former chronicle and Achikishi in the latter.)

The following year, on his recommendation, the scholar Wani (called Wani Kishi in the *Kojiki*) arrived in Japan bringing the *Analects* of Confucius (10 volumes) and the "Thousand-Character Classic" (1 volume). Traditionally, the arrival of Wani is taken as the introduction of Confucianism into Japan. The date 405 (16th year of Emperor Ōjin's reign) is corroborated by Korean documents.

However, to say that Confucianism was imported into Japan with the presentation of the *Analects* to the imperial court in 405 is at best a formality. It is highly probable that prior to that date, with all the comings and goings between Japan and the Chinese mainland and the Korean peninsula, there were people with knowledge of the Confucian classics who had taught the Japanese about them.

■ ■ ■

Daoism (Taoism) is, in short, a Chinese folk religion. The relationship between Confucianism and Daoism is equivalent to the relationship between Japan's Imperial Family Shintō and Yamatoism. Imperial Family Shintō is the form of Shintō which the Imperial Household, supporting the state's authority, believes in.

Consequently, the religion of Daoism was not imported in

キリスト教が伝来するのと同じような形で伝来するわけではありません。なぜなら、道教は「中国人らしい生き方」を教えたものであって、日本人が「中国人らしい生き方」をできるわけがないからです。その意味では、道教は日本に伝来していないのです。

　ただし、たとえば道教に由来する神や信仰、文物などは日本にも伝わり、また日本文化に大きな影響を及ぼしています。たとえば平安時代に伝わった庚申待（かのえさるの日に寝ずに徹夜する習俗）や陰陽道（陰と陽の2原理で吉凶を説明しようとする思想）などに、道教の影響があります。

the same manner that Buddhism or Christianity was. That is because Daoism taught "the Chinese way of living," and there is no way that Japanese could live in the same way that the Chinese did. In that sense, Daoism has not yet been imported into Japan.

However, gods, beliefs and culture that originated in Daoism were introduced to Japan, and it had a great influence on Japanese culture. For example, through the custom, imported during the Heian period, of Kōshinmachi, a festival in which one stays awake all night on *kanoesaru no hi*, and belief in the Way of Yin and Yang (the explaining of good or bad fortune by the two principles of Yin and Yang), Daoism has been influential.

第3章　平安時代

輸入仏教から国産仏教へ

Q❶ 次は平安時代になりますね。

　奈良時代、平安時代、江戸時代といった時代区分は、政治権力の所在地によるものです。奈良時代は奈良の平城京に都があった時代で、710年から784年までです。

　平安時代は、狭義には平安京に都が移された794年から鎌倉幕府が成立する1192年までの400年間になります。しかし、歴史学者のうちには、平安京を開いた桓武天皇の即位の年（781年）を始点とし、源頼朝が鎌倉政権を確立した1185年を終点にしたほうがいいと言う人が多いようです。

　しかし、このような時代区分のほかに、日本史においては「律令時代」といった時代区分があります。これは、701年に制定・施行された「大宝律令」を国家統治の基本法典として国家の運営がなされた時代をいいます。「大宝律令」は散逸して現在は残っていませんが、718年の「養老律令」とほぼ同文だとされています。ともかく律令時代は8世紀から10世紀ごろまで続きました。11世紀になると、次の「荘園時代」に移ります。

CHAPTER 3   HEIAN PERIOD

From Imported Buddhism to Buddhism Made in Japan

❝ **Next comes the Heian period, right?**

The division of periods into Nara period, Heian period, Edo period and so on is based on the location of political power. The Nara period, when the capital of Heijōkyō was in Nara, lasted from 710 to 784.

The Heian period, in the narrow sense, lasted four centuries, from the removal of the capital to Heiankyō in 794 to the establishment of the Kamakura bakufu in 1192. Among historians, however, many take the ascension of Emperor Kanmu in 781 as the starting point and say that the end point was 1185, when Minamoto no Yoritomo established the Kamakura government.

However, in addition to this kind of periodization, there is another periodization called the *ritsuryō jidai*, the period of the *ritsuryō* laws. This refers to the period when the state was ruled by the fundamental legal statutes of the Taihō Code that was established and implemented in 701 for administering the country. The original text of this code has not survived, but it is thought to be similar to the Yōrō Code of 718. At any rate, the *ritsuryō* period continued from the 8th century until about the 10th century. In the 11th century, history moves into the *shōen*

そうすると、平安時代は、前期は律令時代で奈良時代と同じ時代区分になり、後期になって荘園時代になり、前期とは違った時代になります。つまり、平安時代といっても、前期と後期ではだいぶ性格が違っていることに注意しておいてください。

Q❷ では、平安前期の特色を話してください。

　平安前期は、いま述べたように律令時代です。

「律令」というのは、「律」は今日の刑法に相当し、「令」は行政法にあたります。これに「格」(きゃく)（律令の改正条項）と「式」(しき)（律令の施行細則）が加わって、「律令格式」と呼ばれる古代中央集権国家の基本法典が構成されます。
　そこで言いたいことは、律令時代の国家の宗教は、すべて律令によって統制されていたということです。すなわち、「神祇令」(じんぎりょう)によって神職を、「僧尼令」(そうにりょう)によって僧尼を取り締まっています。

　いいですか、「神祇令」も「僧尼令」も「令」ですね。「令」というのは今日でいえば行政法です。これはつまり、神職も僧尼も国家公務員であったことを意味します。国家公務員だからこそ、国家が制定した法律（律令）によって統制されるのです。
　なお、神職といっても、これは官立の神社の神官です。庶民の神社（つまりやまと教の神社。村の鎮守(ちんじゅ)の神様）の神主(かんぬし)ではありません。じつをいえば、

jidai, the period of private estates. That means that the early part of the Heian period belongs to the *ritsuryō* period together with the Nara period, while the latter part, the period of private estates, is a different period. In other words, please be mindful of the fact that even when we use the term Heian period, the early and latter parts are entirely different in character.

❝ So, what are the special features of the early Heian period?

As I have just said, the early part of the Heian period is the *ritsuryō* period.

The *ritsu* of *ritsuryō* refers to what in the present day we call penal laws, and the *ryō* part refers to the administrative laws. With the addition of *kyaku*, articles of amendment, and *shiki*, enforcement regulations, this *ritsuryō kyakushiki* formed the fundamental legal code of the ancient centralized state.

What I would like to say here is that the religions of the state during the *ritsuryō* period were controlled by the *ritsuryō* codes. That is, the Shintō priesthood (*shinshoku*) were regulated by the laws called *Jingi-ryō* and the Buddhist priest and nuns were regulated by laws called *Sōni-ryō*.

Be sure to note that the above are what we today would call administrative laws. This means that the Shintō priests and Buddhist priests and nuns are national public servants. And precisely because they are national government personnel, they are under the regulations of the law (*ritsuryō*).

Moreover, even though they are called priests, they are priests of national shrines. They are not *kannushi* of the shrines of the common people (i.e., shrines of Yamatoism, village tutelary

村の鎮守の神社の神主は、村人のうちの選ばれた長老が就任する輪番制だったのです。これを一年神主とか当年神主といいます。したがって、やまと教でいう神主というのは専業の神主ではないことに注意してください。「神祇令」で取り締まりを受けるのは、官立の神社にいる専業神主だけです。

一方、僧尼のほうは、全員が国家公務員でした。唐僧・鑑真の来朝以後は、国家試験に合格した者だけが受戒して正式の僧尼となることができたのです。もちろん、正式の僧尼には国家から給与に相当するものが支給されます。

このような正式の僧尼に対して、自分勝手に出家して僧尼になった者は「私度僧」と呼ばれます。この私度僧は、律令制が厳格に運用されていた時代には、見つかれば還俗させられました。なぜなら、私度僧になると税金を払わずにすみます。というより、税金を払わずにすむように、自分勝手に村を出て私度僧になるのです。政府としてはそれは困りますから、私度僧は見つかれば元の村に帰されたのです。けれども、律令制が崩れた時代になると、私度僧が数多くなり、野放し状態になりました。ただし、律令制が機能しなくなるのは平安後期になってからです。

＊

さて、平安前期は律令時代で、その意味では奈良

shrines). Actually, the priest of the shrine of the guardian deity of a village was selected from among the elders within the village, and these priests served on a rotation system. That is what the terms *ichinen kannushi* ("one-year priest") and *tōnen kannushi* ("current-year priest") refer to. Be sure to note that as a result of this, the "priest" of Yamatoism is not a priest by profession. The priests that fall under the control of the *Jingiryō* code are only the professional priests at the national government shrines.

As for the Buddhist priests and nuns, they were all public servants. Following the arrival of the T'ang priest Ganjin, only those who passed a national examination were formally ordained into the priesthood. For these official priests and nuns, a grant was provided by the state that was the equivalent of wages.

In contrast with these official priests and nuns, a person who of his own free will renounced the world was called an "unofficial priest." Such "self-declared priests," during periods when the *ritsuryō* system was rigorously enforced, if found, would be forced to return to secular life, because if one became such an unofficial priest, one could gain exemption from paying taxes. That is to say, a person could leave a village on his own initiative and become a self-proclaimed priest in order to avoid paying taxes. From the government's stance, this would be troublesome, so if such unofficial priests were found, they would be sent back to their original village. However, when the *ritsuryō* system collapsed, such priests increased in number and they were free to act as they wanted. The system ceased to function after the latter part of the Heian period.

▪ ▪ ▪

The early part of the Heian period was a continuation of the

時代に連続しています。そして、この律令時代は国家仏教の時代です。僧尼は国家公務員で、その仕事は国家の安泰を祈ることです。読者は不思議に思われるかもしれませんが、「僧尼令」は僧尼が一般庶民と接触することを禁じています。その理由は、僧尼が民衆の指導者となって、国家権力に刃向かってくるのを恐れたためだと思われます。

　それはともかく、たしかに奈良時代と平安前期とは連続していますが、連続だけではなしに断絶もあります。つまり、平安時代は大きく奈良時代と違っているところもあるのです。

　奈良仏教は、前章にも述べましたが、あまりにも政治と癒着していました。桓武天皇（在位781-806）は784年にそれまでの平城京を捨てて、山背国（やましろのくに）（京都府）の長岡京へ遷都しましたが、それは仏教と政治の癒着を断つためでした。もっとも、この長岡京への遷都は失敗に終わり、10年後の794年に平安京へ再遷都しています。だが、ともかく桓武天皇は、奈良の寺を平安京に一寺も移転させていません。この桓武天皇の政治姿勢こそが、奈良時代と平安時代の二つの時代を分かつものだと言えるでしょう。

Q❸ 平安時代の仏教界の二大スターといえば、最澄（さいちょう）と空海（くうかい）ですね。

　平安時代の最初の天皇である桓武天皇の信任を得た僧が最澄（767-822）です。

ritsuryō period, in that sense continuing the Nara period. And the *ritsuryō* period was one of state Buddhism. Priests and nuns were national public servants and their work was to pray for the security of the country. The reader may find it strange, but the *Sōniryō* forbade the priests and nuns to come into contact with the common people. This may have been due to fear that if such a person became a leader among the common people, he might resist the authority of the state.

Whatever the case, while it is true that the Nara period and Heian period were a continuation, there was also some discontinuity. That is, in some ways Heian was very different from the Nara period.

As I said in the previous chapter, Nara Buddhism had an overly cozy relationship with political administrators. In 784, Emperor Kanmu (reigned 781–806) abandoned the capital at Heijōkyō and transferred it to Nagaokakyō in Yamashiro province (present-day Kyōto prefecture), doing so in order to break up the collusive ties between Buddhism and the government. Though the transfer to Nagaoka ended in failure, a decade later in 794, the capital was moved to Heiankyō. Despite everything, Kanmu permitted not a single Nara temple to be transferred to Heiankyō. It can be said that it was Emperor Kanmu's political stance that divided the Nara and Heian periods into two separate periods.

> **Saichō and Kūkai could be called the two superstars of Heian Buddhism, couldn't they?**

The priest who obtained the confidence of Emperor Kanmu, first emperor of the Heian period, was Saichō (767–822).

最澄は19歳（一説では20歳）で奈良の東大寺で受戒したのち、すぐさま比叡山に入山しました。その比叡山にあって彼は中国の天台の教えに出会い、『法華経』を中心とする天台の教学をみずからの宗旨としました。

　桓武天皇は、政治と癒着し、堕落してしまった奈良仏教には失望しましたが、仏教そのものを見限ったわけではありません。むしろ日本の新しい時代を担える真の仏教を求めていました。最澄もまた、時代の流れを正確に読み取り、新しい時代には「新しい仏教」がなければならないと考え、あらゆる仏教の教えを統合する経典として『法華経』を位置づけ、『法華経』にもとづく天台の教学を学んだのです。ここに桓武天皇と最澄の考えが一致し、最澄は桓武天皇の信任を得て、日本に天台宗という新しい宗派を開きました。

　なお、最澄はまじめな人柄であって、日本に天台宗を開く前に、804年にみずから唐に渡って、中国の天台山において天台教学を学んでいます。そして帰朝後の806年に新しい宗派を開いたのです。

最澄

Q❹ しかし最澄は、中国において密教も学んだのではありませんか？

　じつは最澄が開いた天台宗の教学は、中国においてはいささか時代遅れであったことは否めません。もっとも、これは日本の地理的環境の然らしめるところであって、最澄の責任ではありません。当時の中国で最先端の仏教といえば密教でした。その密教

At the age of 19 (some say 20), Saichō became a disciple of Buddha at Tōdaiji in Nara and promptly went to live in the monastery on Mt. Hiei. There he encountered T'ien-t'ai teachings from China and took as his own occupation learning the teachings of the sect which centered on the Lotus Sutra.

Emperor Kanmu had lost hope in Nara Buddhism because of its collusion with politics and its corruption, but that did not mean he had abandoned Buddhism itself. Instead, he was searching for a true form of Buddhism that could support a new era. Saichō, too, accurately read the current of the times, and thinking that a new era required a "new Buddhism," determining that the Lotus Sutra was the sutra which unified all the teachings of Buddhism, he learned the T'ien-t'ai teachings, which were based on that scripture. In this, Emperor Kanmu's thinking and Saichō's thinking corresponded, and so Saichō earned Kanmu's confidence and established Tendai as a new sect of Japanese Buddhism.

Being of serious character, before establishing the Tendai sect, Saichō himself traveled to T'ang China in 804 to study T'ien-t'ai sect doctrines on Mt. T'ien-t'ai. When he returned to Japan in 806, he founded the new Tendai sect.

❝ But didn't Saichō also study esoteric Buddhism in China?

Actually the teachings of the Tendai sect founded by Saichō were undeniably slightly behind the times in China. This was not Saichō's fault, but due rather to Japan's geographical situation. At that time, the leading edge of Buddhism was esoteric Buddhism. Just prior to returning to Japan, Saichō had briefly

を、最澄は帰国する直前に、ほんの少し学びました。

　そして帰国後、最澄は桓武天皇のためにその密教の儀式を行いました。怨霊に苦しんでいる桓武天皇を救うためです。桓武天皇は時代の最先端を行くその密教の儀式を喜び、最澄が開いた天台宗においても、天台教学とともに密教をも学ぶようにと命じました。

　だが、最澄にすれば、それは困ります。なぜなら、彼は密教をほんの少ししか学んでいないからです。そこで最澄は、このあとすぐに解説することにしている空海に協力を求めようとしました。けれども、最澄と空海は、密教というものに対する考え方が百八十度違っています。そのため空海の協力は得られず、天台宗の密教は最澄が生きていたころは中途半端に終わってしまいます。

　ところで、天台宗の密教を「台密」といいます。それに対して空海が開いた真言宗の密教を「東密」と呼びます。で、台密を完成させたのは、最澄の没後に中国に渡って密教を学んだ円仁（794-864）です。その後、円珍（814-891）も中国に渡って密教を学んできました。

　さて、話を元に戻して最澄ですが、彼は比叡山を仏教の総合大学にしたかったようです。天台教学においては、もともと『法華経』が仏教のあらゆる教えを統合・総合するものと考えられています。したがって、『法華経』を学ぶことによって、仏教のすべてが学べるのだというのが天台宗の主張です。それゆえなんでしょうが、後世、比叡山という総合大学からは数多の卒業生が輩出し、日本の仏教界を賑わしています。少しリスト・アップしておきます。

encountered and studied about esoteric Buddhism.

Upon returning to Japan, Saichō performed an esoteric Buddhist ceremony for Emperor Kanmu. Its purpose was to save the emperor from a vengeful spirit. Delighted with the ceremony which was the leading edge of the era, Kanmu ordered Saichō to study esoteric doctrines as well as T'ien-t'ai doctrines within the new sect that he had founded.

From Saichō's position, however, this was problematic, because he had learned only a little bit about esoteric teachings. Therefore, Saichō sought the cooperation of Kūkai, whom we will discuss in a moment. However, Saichō and Kūkai had radically different views of esoteric teachings. For that reason, Saichō was unable to obtain Kūkai's cooperation, and during Saichō's lifetime, the Tendai sect's studies of esoteric Buddhism was only halfhearted.

Within the Tendai sect, esoteric Buddhism is referred to as *taimitsu*. In contrast, the Shingon sect which Kūkai founded refers to esoteric teachings as *tōmitsu*. *Taimitsu* was perfected by Ennin (794–864), who went to China after Saichō's death in order to study esoteric learning. Later, Enchin (814–891) also traveled to China to study esoteric Buddhism.

Returning to our main story, Saichō apparently wanted to turn Mt. Hiei into a comprehensive university for Buddhist studies. Within the teachings of Tendai, it had always been held that the Lotus Sutra integrated and synthesized all of the teachings of Buddhism. Therefore, by studying the Lotus Sutra, the Tendai sect asserted, one learned the essence of Buddhism. As a consequence, in later years the "comprehensive university" on Mt. Hiei produced a large number of graduates, enlivening the Japanese Buddhism world. Here let us make a short list of these figures.

源信(942-1017)……『往生要集』を著して浄土教の理論的基礎を築いた天台宗の学僧。

　良忍(1072-1132)……融通念仏宗の開祖。

　法然(1133-1212)……浄土宗の開祖。

　栄西(1141-1215)……臨済宗の開祖。

　親鸞(1173-1262)……浄土真宗の開祖。

　道元(1200-53)……曹洞宗の開祖。

　日蓮(1222-82)……日蓮宗の開祖。

　こうしてみると、比叡山は日本仏教のふるさとだといえそうですね。

■ ■ ■

　それはともかく、最澄が開いた天台宗は、律令制の国家の仏教であり、「国家仏教」でありました。その意味では、奈良時代の仏教とそれほど違いはありません。ただ両者の違いは、奈良仏教が「輸入仏教」であったのに対して、平安仏教は「国産仏教」であったことです。

　輸入仏教というのは、日本人のニーズ（需要）と関係なしに、中国大陸のほうから一方的に日本に「仏教」を送ってくるのです。これは、6世紀の半ばに日本に仏教が伝来した最初のときからそうでした。日本人が求めてもいないのに、「このような宗教がありますよ。どうです、受け容れてみたら」といったかたちで、中国大陸（最初のときは朝鮮半島）から仏教が伝わって来たのです。

Genshin (942–1017)—writer of the *Ōjō Yōshū* (Essentials of Rebirth) and Tendai sect scholar-monk who constructed the theoretical basis for Pure Land (Jōdo) practices

Ryōnin (1072–1132)—founder of the *Yūzū Nenbutsu* sect

Hōnen (1133–1212)—founder of the Pure Land sect

Eisai (1141–1215)—founder of the Rinzai sect

Shinran (1173–1262)—founder of the Pure Land Shin sect

Dōgen (1200–53)—founder of the Sōtō sect

Nichiren (1222–82)—founder of the Nichiren sect

From the above, it would seem that Mt. Hiei is the birthplace of Japanese Buddhism.

■ ■ ■

In any case, the Tendai sect founded by Saichō is Buddhism of the *ritsuryō* system state, or state Buddhism. In that sense, it was not that different from Buddhism of the Nara period. But one difference between the two was Nara Buddhism was "imported" while Heian Buddhism was "homegrown."

"Imported Buddhism" refers to the Buddhism which was one-sidedly sent to Japan from the Chinese mainland without any relation to the needs of the Japanese people. This was true of Buddhism from the very first introduction in the mid-6th century. Even though the Japanese did not ask for it, Buddhism was imported from China (via the Korean peninsula) in the form of "Here's a great religion. How about adopting it?"

それから平安時代になって、日本人自身が、日本にはこのような仏教が必要なんだと考えて、中国に渡って求めている仏教を持ち帰って来るようになったのです。その点が大きな違いになります。

Q❺ では次に、空海について話してください。

空海（774-835）は、最澄と同じ遣唐使(けんとうし)船団に乗って中国に渡りました。同じ船団といっても、4隻が日本から中国に向かって出航したもので、2人の乗った船は違っています。じつはその4隻の遣唐使船団のうち、最澄と空海が乗った2隻だけが無事に中国に着いたもので（ただし着岸した港は違っています）、そのことは日本仏教にとって大きな幸運でした。どちらかの船が沈んでいたり、あるいは両船ともが沈んでいたりすれば、その後の日本仏教の展開は大きく違っていたと思われます。

空海が中国に渡ったのは31歳のときですが、渡航以前の空海が正式の僧であったか否かは、よく分かりません。正式な僧であったにしても、空海は無名の僧でした。その点は有名人であった最澄とだいぶ違っています。

中国に着いて、最澄は当時は僻地になっていた天台山に行きましたが、空海は唐の都である長安(ちょうあん)（現在の西安）に行きます。そして長安において、恵果(けいか)（746-805）から、『大日経(だいにちきょう)』と『金剛頂経(こんごうちょうきょう)』にもとづく密教を学び、2年あまりの滞在ののち帰国しました。

帰国後の空海は、嵯峨(さが)天皇（在位809-823）の支援を受け、密教の第一人者と

空海

Then the Heian period comes along, and the Japanese themselves, thinking that this sort of Buddhism might be necessary, go to China and bring back the type of Buddhism they are looking for. That is the difference between the two.

❝ Next, could you talk about Kūkai?

Together with Saichō, Kūkai (774–835) traveled to China with one of the official Japanese embassies to T'ang. Although they were members of the same embassy, which consisted of four ships, the two men were on different ships. Of the four ships, only the two carrying Saichō and Kūkai reached Chinese shores safely (although they arrived in separate ports). This was immensely fortunate for Japanese Buddhism. Had either of their respective ships sunk, or if both had sunk, the development of Buddhism in Japan would thereafter have been very different.

Kūkai was 31 when he traveled to China, and it is not clear whether he was an officially ordained priest before going. But even if he was, he was an unknown figure. That was a major contrast with the well-known Saichō.

When he arrived in China, Saichō went to the remote Mt. T'ien-t'ai, but Kūkai went to the T'ang capital of Ch'ang-an (present-day Hsian, Xian). In Ch'ang-an, he studied esoteric Buddhism based on the Sutra of Great Light (Maha Vairocana Sutra) and The Diamond Peak Sutra (Vajrasekhara Sutra) under Keika (Huiguo, Hui-kuo), and a little more than two years later he returned to Japan.

Once he returned, Kūkai received support from Emperor Saga and became active as the foremost authority on esoteric

して活躍します。嵯峨天皇は桓武天皇の皇子ですが、2人の性格はまったく違っていました。桓武天皇は徹頭徹尾の政治家で、それだけに権力闘争に明け暮れ、倒した政敵の怨霊に悩まされたりしています。しかし嵯峨天皇は、政治のほうは摂政にまかせて、みずからは文化人としての人生を送りました。

　その意味では、桓武天皇と最澄、嵯峨天皇と空海の結び付きがおもしろいですね。文化人である嵯峨天皇は、空海が持ち帰った時代の最先端を行く密教の文明的な華やかさに魅せられ、空海の支援者になったのです。もしも嵯峨天皇がいなければ、空海の真言宗の密教は別の展開をしたかもしれません。

　空海は823年に京都洛南の東寺を賜り、ここを真言密教の根本道場にしました。東寺は、現在は新幹線の京都駅の南側に五重塔が見えるあの寺です。それゆえ、真言宗の密教を「東密」と言います。

　それより前、816年に空海は高野山の地を修行の道場として賜っています。けれども、高野山が真言宗の本格的な聖地となったのは空海の没後で、弟子たちの活躍によってでした。

Q❻ 密教とは何ですか？　分かりやすく解説してください。

　仏教は、いまから2600年ほどの昔、インドにおいて釈迦が創唱した宗教です。そして、日本に伝来

Buddhism. Saga was the son of Emperor Kanmu, but they were complete contrasts in terms of character. Emperor Kanmu was a statesman from head to toe, all the more so because he was constantly involved in power struggles and afflicted by the vengeful spirits of the political enemies he toppled. In contrast, Emperor Saga left administration up to his regent, while he himself spent his life as a man of culture.

In that sense, the relationship between Emperor Kanmu and Saichō and that between Emperor Saga and Kūkai are quite interesting. The intellectual Emperor Saga was fascinated with the cultural brilliance of the state-of-the-art esoteric Buddhism that Kūkai had brought back, and he became Kūkai's patron. Without Emperor Saga, it is possible that Kūkai's Shingon sect of esoteric Buddhism would have developed quite differently.

In 823, Kūkai was granted Tōji in the southern part of Kyōto, and he made it the basic center for the study of Shingon esoteric Buddhism. Tōji, literally "Eastern Temple," is on the south side of the Shinkansen Kyōto Station and it has a five-storied pagoda. Because of its name, the teachings of Shingon are called *tōmitsu,* the "eastern esoteric teachings."

Prior to that, in 816, Kūkai had been granted land of Mt. Kōya to use as a religious training center. However, it was after Kūkai's death that through the efforts of his disciples Mt. Kōya became a truely sacred site.

❝ What is esoteric Buddhism in simple terms?

Buddhism is the religion founded some 2,600 years ago by Shakyamuni in India. The Buddhism which was transmitted to

した仏教は、インドから中央アジア、中国および朝鮮半島を経由して伝わったものです。したがって、2600年という時間と、インド、中央アジア、中国などの空間のうちで、仏教はさまざまに変化し、多種多様な仏教が成立しています。密教もそのうちの一つの発展形態ですが、密教だけではなく、仏教にはどのような種類があるかをここで見ておきましょう。

A──大乗仏教・小乗仏教

小乗仏教というのは「出家主義」の仏教です。

じつは、釈迦が教えた仏教は出家主義の仏教ではありません。釈迦は在家の人間でも悟りを開く可能性があると主張していたのですが、釈迦の入滅後に釈迦の直弟子たちが、悟りを開いて究極的に救われるのは、家や職業を捨て、妻子を捨てて出家した者だけであり、在家信者には真の救いがないとする、閉鎖的、独善的な仏教を主張しました。それが小乗仏教です。したがって、小乗仏教とは少数精鋭主義のエリート仏教です。

このような独善的な小乗仏教に反対したのが大乗仏教です。大乗仏教は万人の救いを主張し、在家の人間にも救いの可能性を認めています。いや、出家者よりもむしろ在家信者のほうこそ救われるのだというのが大乗仏教の主張です。

この大乗仏教は、釈迦の入滅後500年ほどして、インドの地において発祥しました。それゆえ、大乗仏教は、歴史的な意味では釈迦が説いた仏教ではありません。

また、大乗仏教は、インドから中央アジアを経て

Japan came from India via Central Asia, China and the Korean peninsula. Consequently over those 2,600 years and over the distance between India and Japan, Buddhism changed in various ways, and diverse forms of Buddhism came into existence. Esoteric Buddhism is one of the forms that developed, but there are others and let us now look at what types there are at this point.

A—Mahayana and Hinayana

Hinayana is "priestly" Buddhism.

Actually, the Buddhism taught by Shakyamuni was not Buddhism for a priesthood of believers. His emphasis was on the possibility that even laypersons could attain enlightenment. But after Shakyamuni entered Nirvana, his direct disciples came to assert that those who would become enlightened and ultimately be saved were those who set aside home and occupation, abandoned wife and child, and became a priest. They advocated a closed, self-righteous form of Buddhism through which a layperson had no chance of obtaining pure salvation. That is Hinayana Buddhism. Consequently, Hinayana is an elitist Buddhism for the select few.

Contrasting with this self-righteous Hinayana form is Mahayana. Mahayana asserts that any person can be saved, acknowledging that it is possible for laypeople to gain salvation. Not only that, Mahayana asserts that it is actually the layperson, rather than the priest, who will be saved.

Mahayana originated in India some five centuries after Shakyamuni entered Nirvana. Therefore, in a historical sense, Mahayana is not what Shakyamuni actually taught.

Further, Mahayana came from India through Central Asia

中国、日本に伝わりました。それに対して小乗仏教は、インドから東南アジアに伝わった仏教です。それゆえ、前者を北方仏教、後者を南方仏教と呼ぶこともあります。

B── 顕教・密教

　小乗仏教においては、釈迦は基本的には歴史的人物と考えられています。人間が悟りを開いて仏陀になり、その悟りの内容を人々に説き教えたというのです。

　それに対して大乗仏教では、根源的な仏として「宇宙仏」を考えます。「宇宙仏」というのはわたしの命名ですが、毘盧舎那仏や大日如来というのが宇宙仏です。宇宙全体にひろがった仏、宇宙の真理そのものである仏、といった存在だと思ってください。

　この宇宙仏は姿なき仏です。時間と空間の上には存在しない仏です。したがって、この宇宙仏の教えはわれわれ人間は聴聞できません。それで、宇宙仏のほうからわれわれ人間のために、1人の分身仏を送り込まれた。人間の姿・形をとった仏を送ってくださって、その分身仏に宇宙仏の教えを語らせられたのです。そして、そのような分身仏が、ほかならぬ釈迦仏です。つまり、釈迦仏は宇宙仏のメッセンジャー・ブッダなのです。大乗仏教はそう考えています。

　で、釈迦仏は人間の言語（具体的にはそれはインドの言葉でした）で説法されます。そこでは真理が「顕現」されています。はっきりと現れているのです。だから、釈迦仏によって説かれた仏教を「顕

and China to Japan. By contrast, Hinayana is a form of Buddhism which was transmitted from India to Southeast Asia. That is why the former is called Northern Buddhism and the latter, Southern Buddhism.

B—Exoteric and Esoteric Buddhism

Within Hinayana, Shakyamuni is considered a historic person. This human being is said to have achieved enlightenment, become a Buddha and preached the content of that enlightenment to other people.

In contrast, within Mahayana, the "cosmic Buddha" (*uchūbutsu*) is seen as the original Buddha. This "cosmic Buddha" is the name I give it, and it refers to both Vairocana Buddha (Birushana butsu) and Mahavairocana (Dainichi Nyorai, the Great Sun). You may think of this as an existence that spreads throughout the entire universe, and this Buddha is the truth of the universe in itself.

This cosmic Buddha is a buddha with no form. It is a buddha which does not exist in time or space. Consequently, we human beings are incapable of hearing the teachings of this cosmic Buddha, so this buddha itself, on behalf of human beings, has sent an incarnation to us. This buddha in human aspect and human form was sent and tells us the teachings of the cosmic Buddha. This incarnation is none other than Shakyamuni, Gautama Buddha. In other words, Shakyamuni is the "messenger buddha" of the cosmic Buddha. This is the Mahayanist way of thought.

The Buddha preached in the language of human beings, or to be more precise, in a language of India. Within that, truth was manifested. It was put into clear form. That is why the teachings preached by Shakyamuni Buddha are called exoteric 開放的な

教(ぎょう)」といいます。この「顕教」に対するものが「密教」です。

「密教」とは何か？　それは、分身仏である釈迦仏の仲介なしに、われわれが直接、宇宙仏の説法を聴聞しようとする仏教です。姿・形のない宇宙仏がどうして説法できるのか!?　そう反問されるかもしれませんが、密教においては、宇宙仏は、

　　──秘密言語あるいは象徴言語──

でもって説法しておられると考えます。秘密言語・象徴言語というのは、いわば言語ならざる言語です。それとも暗号といえばよいでしょうか。普通にはわれわれはそれを聞くことはできませんが、人間が宇宙の真理に溶け込んでしまえば、あるいは宇宙の真理と一心同体になってしまえば、その秘密言語が聞こえるようになる。密教はそう考えています。

C──自力仏教・他力仏教

　仏教においては、われわれが住んでいるこの世界を"娑婆(しゃば)"と呼びます。娑婆は煩悩(ぼんのう)の世界です。苦しみや悩みが絶えない世界です。

　この娑婆の反対が仏の世界です。悟りの世界です。仏の世界には苦しみも悩みもありません。そこで仏の世界を"浄土(じょうど)"と呼びます。あるいは"仏国土(ぶっこくど)"ともいいます。

　いま浄土（仏国土）からわれわれの娑婆世界に1本の太いロープが降ろされてきました。われわれはそのロープを手繰(たぐ)り昇って行けば、浄土に達することができます。つまり、悟りが開けるのです。仏教というのは、わたしたちがロープを手繰り昇って悟りの世界（浄土）に到達することを目指していま

Buddhism. Contrasting with "exoteric Buddhism" is "esoteric 秘密の
Buddhism."

What is esoteric Buddhism? It is the teaching of the preaching that we attempt to hear directly from the cosmic Buddha, without the mediation of Shakyamuni Buddha. How can the cosmic Buddha who has no form or shape possibly preach the Dharma 法? One may certainly ask that question in return. But in esoteric Buddhism, it is believed that the cosmic Buddha preaches the Dharma in "secret language" or "symbolic language." Whether secret or symbolic, it is as it were "language without language." Or perhaps we could call it a code 暗号. Normally, we are unable to hear it, but if a human being harmonizes with the truth of the universe, or merges 溶け込む as one with that universal truth, one will be able to hear that secret language. Esoteric Buddhism believes this.

C—Buddhism of *jiriki* (self-power) and Buddhism of *tariki* (nonself-power)

In Buddhism, the place where we humans live is called *shaba*, "this world." It is a world of *bonnō*, earthly passions, a world where suffering 苦しみ and anguish 悩み are never-ending.

The opposite of "this world" is the world of the buddhas, the world of enlightenment. In the world of the buddhas, there is neither suffering nor anguish. So the world of the buddhas is called the Pure Land, *Jōdo*, or *Bukkokudo*.

Now then, a single thick rope has just been lowered from the Pure Land to this *shaba* world of ours. If we can pull ourselves hand over hand up that rope, we can reach the Pure Land. That is, we can experience enlightenment. Buddhism takes as its aim our climbing up that rope and reaching the "other world" of the Pure Land. One climbs the rope with one's own strength and

す。自分の力で一生懸命昇るのだから、それを「自力仏教」といいます。

　けれども、ロープを手繰り昇る能力のない人はどうすればいいのでしょうか……？　能力がない、もしくは低いのだから、あきらめるよりほかなさそうです。

　でも、そのような低能力、無能力の人を見放してしまえば、仏教は万人の救いではなくなってしまいます。まあ、小乗仏教の考え方だと、小乗仏教は本質的にエリートのための仏教ですから、見放してもいいかもしれませんが、大乗仏教の精神からすれば、見放すことはできません。そこで大乗仏教では、能力の劣った人のための救いとして、仏の慈悲による救いが考えだされました。

　それは、比喩的にいえば、仏の世界から降ろされてきたロープを自分のからだに巻き付ける方法です。ロープをからだに巻き付ければ、あとは仏のほうでウィンチでもってロープを巻き揚げてくださるのです。そういう理論が考えだされました。そしてそういう考え方を、他力仏教といいます。

　自力仏教・他力仏教というのは、そういう考え方の差にもとづいています。

　ただし、自力仏教といっても、100パーセント自分の力で救われるのではありません。100パーセントの自力であれば、それは宗教ではないからです。自力仏教においてロープを手繰り昇る、そのロープそのものは仏の世界から降ろされてきたものです。そこには仏の力が働いています。

　わたしは、この自力と他力との差を、
　――猿の道・猫の道――
　でもって説明しています。外敵が襲ってきたと

with all one's might, so this is called self-power Buddhism.

However, what about those people who do not have the ability to climb up on their own? Since they either do not have the ability or at least not enough ability, then all they can do is give up.

But if Buddhism gives up on those with little or no ability, then it cannot save everyone. Of course, from the Hinayana viewpoint, Buddhism is essentially intended for the elite, so giving up on the others is no problem. However, the spirit of Mahayana Buddhism cannot give up on the others. That is why Mahayana came up with salvation through the compassion of the Buddha for those with lesser abilities.

Metaphorically speaking, that is the method of taking the rope that has been lowered from the world of the Buddha and wrapping it around one's body. Once the rope is tied, the Buddha simply uses a winch to hoist the person up. That's the theory that was worked out.

Jiriki (self-power) Buddhism and *tariki* (nonself-power) Buddhism are based on this kind of thinking.

However, even within *jiriki* Buddhism, one cannot be saved 100 percent by one's own powers. If you could do everything with your own powers, there would be no religion. Even in *jiriki* Buddhism, if you climb that rope hand over hand, the rope itself has previously been lowered from the land of the Buddha. Buddha's powers are at work in this.

I usually explain the difference between *jiriki* and *tariki* as the "way of the monkey" and the "way of the cat." When an external threat appears, a baby monkey clings with all its might

き、仔猿は母猿の腹にしがみつき、そして母猿が仔猿を連れて逃げます。母猿を仏だとすれば、仔猿は仏によって救われるのですが、仔猿は少なくとも「しがみつく」といった自力の行為をしています。

それに対して猫の場合は、母猫が仔猫の首をくわえて運び去ります。仔猫はまったく何もせず、ただ母猫（＝仏）にまかせている。それが他力だと思ってください。

つまり、すべて根底には仏の力があって、その仏の上での自力・他力なのです。その点をまちがえないように。

Q❼ 他力仏教は誰によって説かれたのですか……？

他力仏教というのはわたしの命名であって、一般にはこれを、

——浄土教——

といいます。日本の仏教史において、浄土教の教えを広めた最初の人は法然（1133–1212）です。

最澄・空海の平安前期から一気に平安後期の法然に飛んでしまいましたが、この３人には大きな共通点があります。それは、仏教の「選択」をしたことです。すなわち最澄は、日本にふさわしい仏教は小乗仏教ではなく大乗仏教であると「選択」をし、空海は顕教よりも密教のほうが優れた仏教であると「選択」をしました。そして法然は、自力仏教よりも他力仏教（浄土教）こそが、日本の民衆にとって必要な仏教であると「選択」したのです。

じつは法然の没年は鎌倉時代になります。それゆえ法然を鎌倉時代の仏教者に位置づける学者もいま

to its mother's belly and the mother escapes together with her baby. If we see the mother monkey as a *hotoke*, then the baby monkey is saved by the mother, but is still carrying out the *jiriki* action of clinging.

In contrast, in the case of cats, the mother cat takes its baby's neck between its teeth. The kitten does not have to do a single thing, except leave everything up to the mother cat, the *hotoke*. You can think of this method as *tariki*.

In other words, the power of Buddha underlies everything. Both *jiriki* and *tariki* are founded on the Buddha. Be sure not to misconstrue that.

❝ Who preached "nonself-power" Buddhism?

"Nonself-power" (*tariki*) Buddhism is what I call it, although people generally called it Pure Land Buddhism. In the history of Japanese Buddhism, the first person to spread the teachings of the Pure Land was Hōnen (1133–1212).

We have jumped immediately from Saichō and Kūkai of the early Heian period to Hōnen in the late Heian period, but there is a major common feature shared by the three. That is, they each made a "choice" in Buddhism. Saichō appropriately chose Mahayana and not Hinayana as the form of Buddhism that suited Japan. Kūkai chose esoteric rather than exoteric Buddhism as the superior form. Hōnen chose "nonself-power" (Jōdo) Buddhism rather than "self-power" Buddhism as essential for the Japanese people.

As it happens, the year of Hōnen's death fell within the Kamakura period. As a result, some scholars place Hōnen

すが、わたしは、法然がそのような「選択」をした年代は平安時代であり、また平安仏教の特色は何よりも仏教の「選択」をしたことにあるのだから、法然を平安時代の仏教者として位置づけています。

　さて、法然の「選択」は、民衆の立場に立っての仏教の選びです。最澄と空海は、日本国という国家の立場から、小乗仏教よりも大乗仏教が、顕教よりも密教が優れているといって、それぞれ大乗仏教と密教を選択しました。国家の安泰を祈るための選択です。

　だが、法然の「選択」はそうではありません。法然は、自力仏教よりも他力仏教（浄土教）のほうが優れていると考えたのではありません。優れているということでいえば、自力仏教のほうが優れているでしょう。自力仏教は"聖道門"と呼ばれているように、こちらのほうが正統派なんです。

　法然の主張は、いくら優れた仏教であっても、貧しく愚かな民衆がそれによって救われないのであれば、民衆にはそのような仏教は役に立たない。民衆に役に立つ仏教は、他力仏教であり、浄土教なんだ、というものです。

　そこでわたしは、法然による「選択」を、
　　——メーカーの論理からユーザーの論理へ——
の転換であったと表現しています。生産者側からすれば立派な製品であっても、それを購入する資力のない者には役に立ちません。ユーザーは自分の資力でもって購入できるものを求めているのです。法然は、浄土教こそが民衆の救いになる仏教だと主張したのです。

法然

among the Buddhist figures of the Kamakura period, but I believe Hōnen belongs to Heian period, because he made his choice in this period, and moreover the distinctive feature of Heian Buddhism was the making of these choices.

The "choice"—"selection"—that Hōnen made was to single out a form of Buddhism that took into account the standpoint of the ordinary person. Saichō and Kūkai made their respective choices from the standpoint of the Japanese state. They chose, respectively, Mahayana over Hinayana and esoteric over exoteric. Their selections were made out of hopes for the peace and security of the nation.

But that was not true for Hōnen. He did *not* believe that "nonself-power Buddhism" (Jōdo teachings) was *superior* to "self-power Buddhism." In terms of superiority, surely "self-power Buddhism" wins the contest. "Self-power Buddhism," known as "the gate to the Holy Path of Buddhism," is the orthodox school.

Hōnen held that regardless of how superior a form of Buddhism it was, if the poor, simple common people could not gain salvation through it, then such Buddhism was of no use to the masses. The Buddhism that would be of service to ordinary people was "nonself-power Buddhism," the teachings of the Pure Land.

I refer to the choice that Hōnen made as the switch from "logic of the manufacturer" to "logic of the user." What may be a superb product in the eyes of the producer is of no use at all to a person who does not have the financial resources to buy it. The user looks for something he or she can buy with what he or she has. Hōnen insisted that it was precisely the teachings of the Pure Land that would become a salvation for the people in general.

法然が開いた新しい宗派を浄土宗といいます。この浄土宗においては、われわれが「南無阿弥陀仏」と称えれば、阿弥陀仏のほうから救いの手を差し伸べてくださり、死後には阿弥陀仏がおられる極楽世界に往き生まれることができるとされています。「南無阿弥陀仏」とは、阿弥陀仏に帰依しますという信仰告白であり、すべてを阿弥陀仏におまかせしますという決意表明です。ただ「南無阿弥陀仏」と称えるだけで救われるのですから、貧しく愚かな庶民でも救われるわけです。

　このような法然の浄土教によって、日本に伝来した仏教が、為政者のための国家仏教から民衆のための仏教になることができました。そうしてその浄土教が、燎原の火のごとくに日本全国に広まったのです。

Q❽ 末法思想とは何ですか？

　現代のわれわれが抱いている歴史観は発展型のそれです。歴史というものは、どこまでも進歩・発展・向上するものだと考えられています。

　それに対して仏教の歴史観は、衰退型のそれです。

　仏教は釈迦によって教えられたものですが、釈迦が入滅してしばらくのあいだ（500年か1000年）は、正しい教えが伝わり、また正しい教えによって修行する人がおり、修行の結果悟りを得る人もいます。その時代を正法の時代といいます。

The new sect Hōnen founded is called the Pure Land sect. Within the Pure Land sect it is held that if one chants "*Namu Amida Butsu*" ("I sincerely believe in Amida Buddha [Amitabha]"), Amida will extend the hand of salvation to us, and when we die we will be able to be reborn in the Pure Land of Amida Buddha. "*Namu Amida Butsu*" is a confession of faith that one has become a believer in Amida Buddha and a declaration of resolve to leave everything to Amida. Since all one has to do is to chant "*Namu Amida Butsu*" in order to be saved, even simple, ordinary folk can be saved.

As a result of the Pure Land teachings of Hōnen, the Buddhism that was introduced to Japan changed from being state Buddhism for those who administered the country to Buddhism for the people. That Pure Land teaching spread like wildfire throughout the country.

❝ What is the concept of the Decay of the Law (*Mappō*)?

Our present-day view of history is a developmental type. History is seen as something that progresses, develops and advances continuously.

In contrast, the Buddhist view of history is one of atrophy, degeneration and decline.

Buddhism was taught by Shakyamuni, and for a while after he entered Nirvana (either 500 or 1,000 years), the correct teachings were transmitted, people trained themselves according to the proper teachings, and some were able to attain enlightenment as a result of their ascetic practices. This is called the period of *shōbō*, the Righteous Law.

その正法の時代が500年あるいは1000年続いたあと、次に像法の時代になります。"像"とはイミテーション、あるいはコピーの意味です。この時代になると、正しい教えがあり、修行者もいますが、悟りを開く人がなくなります。この像法の時代も500年あるいは1000年続きます。

　そのあと、時代は末法時代に入ります。末法時代には正しい教えだけが残り、修行者も悟りを開く人もなくなります。

　末法時代が1万年続くと、最後には法滅の時代になります。そうすると仏教の教えすらなくなってしまうのです。

　これが仏教の歴史観で、わが国では最澄がこの末法思想を提唱したとされています。ただし、それを否定する学者もいます。

　また、わが国では、1052年に末法時代に入ったと考えられています。したがって、平安末期から鎌倉時代にかけての仏教者たちは、この末法思想の影響を大きく受けています。

Q❾ 本地垂迹説とは何ですか？

　インド仏教における神の地位はきわめて低いものでした。すなわち、インド人は、

——天・人・修羅・畜生・餓鬼・地獄——

といった六つの世界を考え、これを「六道輪廻」

After this period of 500 or 1,000 years comes the period of *zōbō*, the Imitative Law. This is a period of "imitation" and "copying." In this period, there are correct teachings and practitioners, but no one attains enlightenment. This period also lasts 500 or 1,000 years.

Following that comes the period of *Mappō*, the Decay of the Law. In this period, only the teachings remain and no one practices or attains enlightenment.

The period of the Decay of the Law continues 10,000 years and finally comes the period of *Hōmetsu*, the period of the Extinction of the Law. This is when even the teachings of the Buddha disappear.

The above is the Buddhist vision of history, and in Japan, it is said that Saichō was the one who advanced the pessimistic theory of the latter days of the Buddhist law. Some scholars, however, disagree with this view.

Further, in Japan it was believed that the year 1052 marked the beginning of this period of *Mappō*. As a result, the Buddhists of the late Heian period through the early Kamakura period were greatly influenced by this concept of the Decay of the Law.

66 What is the *honji suijaku* theory?

In Indian Buddhism, the deities were of very low status. The people of contemporary India believed there were six worlds:
—the world of heavenly beings, the world of human beings, the world of *ashuras* (demons), the world of animals, the world of hungry spirits, hells—

They believed in *rokudō rinne*, transmigration in the six

と呼び、迷える生類がこの六つの世界を輪廻転生するとしたのです。この天界が神々の世界です。まあ、天界は人間世界より少しはましですが、その本質は苦しみの世界であり、迷いの世界です。それに対して仏は、この輪廻の世界から飛び出て、もはや輪廻することのない絶対者です。

しかし、日本の神は、そういう迷いの存在ではありません。もっとも、日本の神々のうちには福の神や貧乏神のようにインドの神（天）と同じ性格の神もいますが、それよりはもう一段高い神もいます。

とくに7世紀の後半になって天皇を中心とした国家体制が整備されると、天皇家の氏神であるアマテラスオオミカミ（天照大神）を頂点とする神々のヒエラルヒー（位階制）が確立します。

そうすると、アマテラスオオミカミのような偉い神を、インド的な仏教理論にもとづいて低級扱いすることができなくなります。そこで考え出された理論が本地垂迹説です。

これは、本地（本源の姿）である仏が、神の姿をとって垂迹（仮の姿をとって現れること）したといった考え方です。この仮の姿をとって現れることを権現ともいいます。権に神になって現れるという意味です。その結果、アマテラスオオミカミの本地として大日如来、熊野権現の本地として阿弥陀如来が設定されています。

この本地垂迹説は、仏教と神道をうまく習合させるための神仏習合思想によるものです。しかし、本地垂迹説はあくまでも仏教のほうにイニシアティヴ

lower worlds, and that animate beings wandered through the six worlds by way of the transmigration of the soul. Heaven is the world of the gods. This world is better than the world of human beings, but essentially it is a world of suffering and illusion. In comparison, a buddha is an absolute being who has broken out of the cycle of rebirth and who will never be reborn again.

However, the Japanese gods are not such beings of illusion. Of course, among Japanese gods are some like the god of good fortune and the god of poverty which have the same character as the gods of India. But other Japanese gods are a step higher in status.

Especially in the latter half of the 7th century, when the system of the nation was being established centered around the emperor, the guardian deity of the Imperial House, Amaterasu Ōmikami, was established at the top of the hierarchy of deities.

A remarkable deity such as Amaterasu surely could not be treated with the low esteem afforded by Indian Buddhist thought. At that point, the theory of *honji suijaku* was worked out which said that there was "original prototype and local manifestation."

According to this theory, the Buddha was the "original prototype" who was "manifested" in the form of local deities. The latter temporary manifestation was called *gongen*, an incarnation of the Buddha. This meant that the Buddha appeared for the time being in the form of a god. As a result, the "original prototype" of Amaterasu Ōmikami was established to be Dainichi Nyorai (Dainichi Buddha, Mahavairocana Tathagata) and the "original prototype" of Kumano Gongen was Amida Nyorai.

The theory of *honji suijaku* emerged from a school of thought that sought to syncretize Buddhism and Shintoism by identifying Buddhist figures as Shintō deities. However, the initiative

（主導権）がありますから、鎌倉中期以降になると神道家のほうから不満が出てきて、反本地垂迹説が主張されるようになりました。それによると、日本の神が本地で、仏が垂迹ということになります。

in promoting this theory came from the Buddhist side, so following the middle of the Kamakura period, when dissatisfaction emerged on the Shintō side, a reverse theory was put forth. According to this, the Japanese deities were the "original prototypes" and the buddhas were "manifestations" of the prototypes.

第4章　鎌倉時代

民衆仏教の成立と展開

Q❶　鎌倉時代には、いわゆる「鎌倉新仏教」が成立していますね。

　日本仏教の宗派は、戦前は「十三宗五十六派」と総称されていました。じつは、"宗派"といった言葉は、たんなる「分派」の意味ではなく、大きな教団の分類を意味する"宗"と、その宗の中での小さな流派の分類である"派"を組み合わせたものです。

　だから、たとえば真言宗御室派だとか、浄土真宗本願寺派といったふうになります。十三宗というのは、天台宗だとか臨済宗といった大きな教団が十三あるというのです。

　ただし、これは戦前の話です。戦後は信教の自由によって宗教教団が国家の統制を離れたもので、数多くの宗派が成立しています。

　しかし、ここでは戦前の十三宗を基準に話を進めます。

■■■

　仏教は6世紀の半ばに日本に伝わって来ましたが、最初のころは宗派といったものはありません。

CHAPTER 4 KAMAKURA PERIOD

The Formation and Development of Popular Buddhism

> **What about the so-called new Kamakura sects that were formed during the Kamakura period?**

Prior to World War II, Japanese Buddhist groups were generally referred to as "the 13 *shū* and 56 *ha*." The Japanese term *shūha* is composed of *shū* and *ha*, but it does not refer to the sects (*shū*) and other denominations (*ha*). Rather, the large religious organizations are called sects (*shū*) and the smaller groups within those sects are called schools *(ha)*.

Therefore, one finds *Shingon-shū Omuro-ha* (Shingon sect, Omuro school) and *Jōdo Shin-shū Honganji-ha* (Jōdo Shin sect, Honganji school). The "13 sects" were large religious organizations, including the Tendai sect and Rinzai sect.

But this is the story prior to World War II. Following the war, as a result of the implementation of freedom of religion, religious groups were freed from regulation by the national government, and a large number of sects arose.

Here, however, I will continue the story on the basis of the 13 pre-war sects.

■ ■ ■

Buddhism was transmitted to Japan in the middle of the 6th century, and in the early years it had nothing like sects. The

宗派ができたのは8世紀、奈良時代になってからで、中国から六つの宗が伝えられて来ました。すなわち、法相宗・三論宗・華厳宗・律宗・倶舎宗・成実宗で、これを「南都六宗」と呼びます。もっとも、この六宗は、現在呼ばれている「宗」とだいぶ趣きを異にしていて、「学派」のようなものです。僧侶も特定の宗に属していたわけではありません。

この「南都六宗」のうち、現在まで存続しているのは次の三宗です。
1　華厳宗……大本山は東大寺。
2　法相宗……大本山は興福寺と薬師寺。
3　律宗……本山は唐招提寺。

ついで平安時代になると、前章で述べたように、日本人の手によって新たに二つの宗派が開かれました。
4　天台宗……開祖は最澄。
5　真言宗……開祖は空海。
ここまでの「南都六宗」と天台宗・真言宗を合わせて「旧仏教」と呼びます。

そのあと、平安末期から鎌倉時代にかけて、新たに七宗が成立しました。これが「鎌倉新仏教」と呼ばれるものです。
6　融通念仏宗……良忍（1072-1132）の開創。総本山は大阪市にある大念仏寺。他力仏教（浄土教系の仏教）に属します。
7　浄土宗……開祖は法然。
8　浄土真宗……親鸞（1173-1262）の開宗。
9　時宗……一遍（1239-89）を宗祖とします。総本山は藤沢市にある清浄光寺（俗称は遊

sects appeared in the 8th century, after the beginning of the Nara period, when six schools of Buddhism were transmitted from China. Referred to as the "Six Nara Schools," they consisted of the Hossō, Sanron, Kegon, Ritsu, Kusha and Jōjitsu schools. These six were quite different from what we might call "sects" today and much more like schools of thought. The priests did not "belong to" any of the individual schools.

Of the six Nara schools, the three that continue to exist are the following:
1 Kegon school—Daihonzan at Tōdaiji
2 Hossō school—Daihonzan at Kōfukuji and Yakushiji
3 Ritsu school—Honzan at Tōshōdaiji

To these we add the two sects founded by Japanese as we saw in the previous chapter:
4 Tendai sect—Founded by Saichō
5 Shingon sect—Founded by Kūkai

The six Nara schools together with Tendai and Shingon are referred to as "old Buddhism."

Following that, from the end of the Heian period through the Kamakura period, seven new sects were established. We refer to these as "Kamakura Buddhism" and they include:
6 Yūzū Nenbutsu sect—Founded by Ryōnin (1072–1132). Sōhonzan is Dainenbutsuji in Ōsaka City. Belongs to the "nonself-power Buddhism" (Pure Land Buddhism).
7 Jōdo (Pure Land) sect—Founded by Hōnen
8 Jōdo Shin (True Pure Land) sect—Founded by Shinran (1173–1262)
9 Ji sect—Founded by Ippen (1239–89). Sōhonzan is

行寺）です。一遍は法然の曾孫弟子になります。

10 臨済宗……栄西（1141-1215）が宋に渡って伝えて来ました。

11 曹洞宗……道元（1200-53）が同じく宋から伝えて来ました。曹洞宗には、福井県の永平寺と横浜市の総持寺の、二つの大本山があります。

12 日蓮宗……開祖は日蓮（1222-82）。総本山は身延山（山梨県）にある久遠寺。

室町時代以後は、新しい宗の創立はありません。けれども、江戸時代の初めに、中国から新しく禅系統の仏教が伝えられて来ました。

13 黄檗宗……明の僧の隠元（1592-1673）によって伝えられました。大本山は宇治市の万福寺です。

以上の十三宗が、日本仏教の基本的な宗派です。

Q❷ では、「鎌倉新仏教」の一つ一つを解説してください。最初に融通念仏宗について。

融通念仏宗の開祖の良忍は平安後期の人です。したがって、これを「鎌倉新仏教」に加えるのはおかしいと思います。

また良忍は天台系の人で、比叡山で学んでいます。そして彼の考え方も、天台宗とそれほど大きな違いはありません。だから、われわれはこれを旧仏教に分類したほうがいいと思います。

Shōjōkōji (known as Yugyōji) in Fujisawa City. Ippen is a third-generation disciple of Hōnen.

10 Rinzai sect– Brought from Sung China by Eisai (1141–1215)

11 Sōtō sect– Brought from Sung China by Dōgen (1200–53). Has two Daihonzan, Eiheiji (Fukui prefecture) and Sōjiji (Yokohama City).

12 Nichiren sect– Founded by Nichiren (1222–82). Sōhonzan is Kuonji on Mt. Minobu in Yamanashi Prefecture.

Since the Muromachi period, no new sects have been established. However, at the beginning of the Edo period, a new Zen-related form of Buddhism was transmitted from China:

13 Ōbaku sect– Transmitted by the Ming monk Ingen (1592–1673). The Daihonzan is Manpukuji in Uji City.

The 13 sects above are the fundamental sects of Japanese Buddhism.

66 Would you please begin with the Yūzū Nenbutsu sect and explain each of the sects in detail?

Founder Ryōnin of the Yūzū Nenbutsu sect is a man of the late Heian period. Therefore, I believe it is odd to include it among the new sects of Kamakura Buddhism.

Further, Ryōnin is related to Tendai and studied at Mt. Hiei. His teachings are not that different from those of Tendai. Therefore, it makes more sense to classify this as a form of older Buddhism.

良忍の念仏(「南無阿弥陀仏」と口に称える念仏です)に対する考え方は、「融通」という言葉がぴったりです。一人一人が称える念仏は小さな力しか持ちません。しかし、大勢の人が念仏すれば、その小さな力がまとまって大きな力になります。そして、その大きな力が一人一人に加わってくるのです。その大きな力でもって、われわれは阿弥陀仏の極楽世界に往生できる。良忍はそのように考えたのです。

Q❸ 法然については前章で語られています。次は親鸞ですね。

　親鸞(1173-1262)は法然の弟子です。前章で述べたように、法然は、その当時の時代背景をもとに、いまの時代の日本の民衆を救える仏教は自力仏教ではなく、阿弥陀仏の救済力にもとづく他力仏教だと主張しました。つまり、他力仏教(念仏の仏教。浄土教)を「選択」したのです。そして、その法然の「選択」をより深く理論化したのが弟子の親鸞でした。

　法然が「選択」した他力仏教のメリット(利点)の一つは、

　　　――易行(いぎょう)――

です。普通、仏教の修行といえば、なかなかの難行です。戒律を守り、坐禅をしたり、あるいは布施行や忍辱(にんにく)行(耐え忍ぶこと)をせねばなりません。

　でも、そのような難行だと、貧しく愚かで、日々の生活に追われている庶民には実践できません。そこで法然は、われわれ庶民はただ「南無阿弥陀仏」

The word "yūzū" ("mutually inclusive") is a perfect way of describing the thought behind Ryōnin's *nenbutsu* (intoning "*Namu Amida Butsu*"). The *nenbutsu* that each individual intones has only a little power. However, if large numbers of people intone the *nenbutsu*, that small power will come together as a large power, and that larger power will in turn be added to each individual. With that great strength, one will be able to enter the Buddhist Paradise of Amida Buddha. Ryōnin thought this way.

> **You have spoken of Hōnen in the earlier chapter, so the next is Shinran?**

Shinran (1173–1262) is Hōnen's disciple. As I said earlier, on the basis of the background of those times, Hōnen asserted that the form of Buddhism that could save the ordinary Japanese people was not "self-power Buddhism" but "nonself-power Buddhism." In other words, he chose "nonself-power Buddhism" (Nenbutsu Buddhism, Pure Land Buddhism). And the one who advanced Hōnen's "choice" even further was his disciple Shinran.

One of the merits of Hōnen's choice was "easiness of practice." Usually when one thinks of Buddhism, its practices seem austere. One has to obey the precepts. One has to practice Zen and endure severe practices.

But when it comes to severe practices, the poor, simple common people, who are under pressure from everyday affairs, cannot so easily practice the teachings. Therefore Hōnen stressed

と口に称える易行(易しい行)だけで救われるのだ、といった主張をしました。

たしかに法然の主張は、従来の仏教の考え方を根底から引っ繰り返す革命的な理論でした。

しかし、それでも、やはり「行」は残っています。いくら易しい行だといっても、われわれはそれを実践せねばなりません。そして、実践が義務づけられると、その実践ができない人が阿弥陀仏の救済力から見放されてしまいます。

そこのところを乗り越えようとしたのが親鸞でした。

親鸞の考え方は、『歎異抄』(この書は、親鸞の弟子唯円が師の言葉をまとめたものです)の中にある次の言葉によって明らかにされています。

《弥陀の誓願不思議にたすけられまひらせて往生をばとぐるなりと信じて、念仏まふさんとおもひたつこゝろのおこるとき、すなはち摂取不捨の利益にあづけしめたまふなり》

[阿弥陀仏の誓願の不思議な力にたすけられて、わたしのような凡夫でも必ず往生できるのだと信じて、お念仏を称えようと思う心が起きたらその瞬間、わたしたちはもれなく阿弥陀仏のお浄土に救いとられているのである]

これによると、われわれは阿弥陀仏の救いを信じて、「南無阿弥陀仏」と念仏を称えようと思った瞬間に救われているのです。実践(行)より先に救いがあるのですから、行は不要になります。ただ阿弥陀仏の救いを信ずればいい。親鸞はそう考えました。したがって、彼においては、易行すら必要なく、信だけがあればよいことになります。

なお、親鸞自身は自分で新たな宗派を開く意思

that the common people could be saved through the easy practice of simply intoning "*Namu Amida Butsu.*"

Clearly Hōnen's assertion is a revolutionary idea which overturned the conventional foundation of Buddhism.

Nonetheless, the idea of "practice" remains. No matter how easy a practice it may be, we at least have to do that much. And if that practice is compulsory, then those who do not carry it out will have to give up on attaining the saving power of Amida Buddha.

It was Shinran who sought to overcome that.

Shinran's thinking is clear in the following quotation from his *Tannishō*, a compilation of his teachings by his disciples: "The moment we believe that we can be saved and enlightened through the power of Amida's Original Vow, and conceive the desire to call upon his name, he at once deigns to save us, never casting us aside."

[Same as previous paragraph]

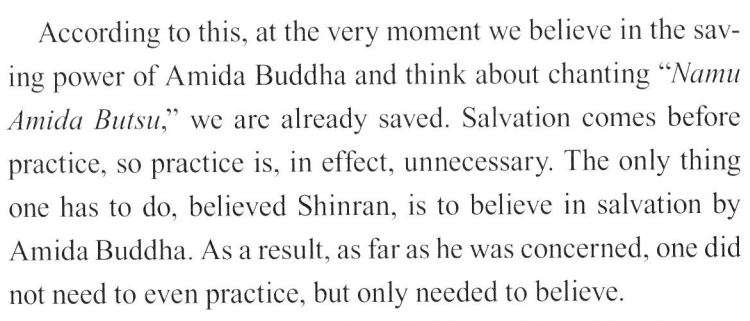

According to this, at the very moment we believe in the saving power of Amida Buddha and think about chanting "*Namu Amida Butsu*," we are already saved. Salvation comes before practice, so practice is, in effect, unnecessary. The only thing one has to do, believed Shinran, is to believe in salvation by Amida Buddha. As a result, as far as he was concerned, one did not need to even practice, but only needed to believe.

Still, it was not the intention of Shinran himself to found a

はありませんでした。彼は、自分は法然の弟子であり、法然の教えから外れていないと思っていました。浄土真宗というのは、親鸞の没後に、親鸞を開祖として後継者たちが独立させた宗派です。

Q❹ 法然も親鸞も、流罪(るざい)になったのではありませんか？

　法然（1133-1212）の教えは、為政者と旧仏教側にとっては好ましくないものでした。前にも述べたように、律令制の下では僧侶は国家公務員であり、僧侶の仕事は国家の安泰を祈ることでありました。あたりまえのことですが、古代の国家にあっては、国家の利益と民衆の利益は相反します。民衆のための法然の仏教は、その意味では国益に反しますから、国家とそれに結びついた旧仏教が、法然に弾圧を加えるのも当然です。

　また、平安後期になると律令制は崩れて、荘園(しょうえん)経済の時代になっています。国家権力を持つものの力は弱まっていますが、多くの荘園を持つ貴族や寺社勢力は、やはり民衆を抑え付けておきたいのです。それゆえ、彼らにとっては法然の教えを黙って見ているわけにはいきません。なぜなら、法然の浄土教によれば、民衆は直接、阿弥陀仏の救いを受けますから、旧仏教を尊崇(そんすう)する必要はありませんし、旧仏教への寄進(きしん)もする必要がないからです。だから、民衆と結びついた法然の浄土教が弾圧を受けたのです。

　そして、その師の法然に連座して弟子たちも弾圧を受け、流罪や死罪になっています。もっとも、弟

new sect. He saw himself as Hōnen's disciple and did not think he was departing from Hōnen's teachings. The Jōdo Shin sect was made independent by his successors, with Shinran as its founder.

66 Were Hōnen and Shinran both banished from the capital?

Hōnen's teachings were not agreeable to the political administrators or to the older forms of Buddhism. As noted earlier, under the *ritsuryō* system, priests were national public servants, and their responsibility was to pray for the security of the nation. Naturally enough, what was beneficial to the ancient state ran counter to the interests of the common people. Hōnen's Buddhism for the people in that sense conflicted with the state's interests. Therefore it was natural that the state—and the older forms of Buddhism tied to it—would suppress Hōnen.

In addition, in the late Heian period, the *ritsuryō* system crumbled, and the period of *shōen* estates began. National power weakened, but the aristocracy, which possessed estates, as well as the authorities of the temples and shrines wanted to keep the common people under control. Therefore, they could not stand by silently and allow Hōnen to teach. The reason is that according to Hōnen's Pure Land teachings, the common people receive the salvation of Amida Buddha directly, without the need to pay reverence to the older Buddhism and without making donations to the older sects. Therefore, Hōnen's Pure Land teachings, which were linked with ordinary people, were suppressed.

The disciples who were implicated with their master Hōnen were suppressed, banished or executed. Not all of them were

子の全員が罪に問われたのではなく、弟子のうちでも過激派であった者が罪に問われています。その代表が親鸞でした。親鸞の思想は、ある意味では仏道修行を全面的に否定するものであったから、旧仏教からすれば極端な過激派に見えたのでしょう。

■■■

なお、このような浄土教に対する弾圧だけではなく、たとえば曹洞宗の開祖の道元も天台宗から弾圧を受けています。しかしこの場合は、新しい宗派が出てくることによって既得権益が侵されることを恐れた旧仏教側からの弾圧であって、あまり政治的なものではなかったように思われます。

また、日蓮も弾圧を受けていますが、これについては後述します。

Q❺ 鎌倉時代には、宋から栄西が臨済宗を伝えています。禅とは何か？ そして栄西はどのような教えを伝えたのですか。

仏道を修行するには、修行者は必ず、

――戒学・定学・慧学の三学――

を修めねばならないとされています。戒学は戒律をしっかりと保つことです。定学は禅定です。坐禅によって心の散乱を防ぎます。慧学とは智慧を身につけることです。ただし、この場合の智慧は、日常生活の中でいう損得の知恵でもないし、ましてや他人を騙すための知恵でもありません。あらゆるものを無差別・平等に見る智慧であって、仏教語ではそれを"般若"と呼びます。

actually accused of wrongdoing, but the extremists among them were. That included Shinran. Shinran's teachings, in one sense, completely denied Buddhism's ascetic practices, and as a consequence, from the viewpoint of older Buddhism, these teachings were radical and extremist.

The Pure Land sect was suppressed and the Tendai sect also suppressed Dōgen, founder of the Sōtō sect. But in the latter case, it was suppression resulting from the fear of the older sect that its previously acquired advantages would be infringed on by the newly emerging sect and was not related to politics.

Nichiren was also suppressed, but we will touch on that later.

❝ In the Kamakura period, Eisai brought the Rinzai sect from Sung China. What is Zen? What kind of teachings did Eisai transmit?

It is held that anyone who follows the path of the Buddha must practice three teachings: the learning of the precepts, learning of meditation and learning of wisdom. Learning of the precepts means the observing of the religious precepts. Learning of meditation means meditative contemplation. Through seated meditation one can ward off the scattering of the mind. Learning of wisdom means the cultivation of wisdom. In this case, wisdom does not refer to the wisdom of advantage and disadvantage in everyday life, and certainly does not mean the kind of wisdom one might put to use in deceiving others. It is the wisdom to see all things without discrimination and all things as equal, which

"般若"とは、「智慧」を意味するサンスクリット語の"プラジュニャー"（その俗語形が"パンニャー"）を音訳したものです。この智慧は、戒学と定学を修めることによって得られるものです。
　このように仏道修行においては「戒・定・慧」の三学が必須徳目であるから、それゆえそのうちの禅定は三分の一になります。なお、"禅""禅定""定""坐禅"はまったく同じ意味です。

　ところが、中国において6世紀の前に菩提達摩（達磨とも表記されます）を初祖とする禅宗が成立しました。菩提達摩はインドから中国に来た僧です。しかし、学者によってはその実在を疑う人もいます。実在したにしても、半ば伝説上の人物です。
　この菩提達摩を初祖とする禅宗においては、坐禅によって直に仏の心が摑めるとし、また実際に仏の心を摑むために坐禅をします。それゆえ、禅宗は「仏心宗」とも呼ばれています。

　そこで、この禅宗あるいは仏心宗においては、坐禅は戒・定・慧の三学の一つではありません。三分の一の定（坐禅）ではなしに、その定のうちに戒があり、また定のうちに慧があるとされています。定がすべてであって、だから一分の一の定と言われています。
　これが禅宗の考え方です。

■ ■ ■

　さて、栄西（1141-1215）ですが、彼は岡山市にある吉備津神社の神官の子として生まれ、比叡山で出家して天台宗の僧となりました。彼の生涯において特筆すべきことは、二度にわたって入宋し

in Buddhism is referred to as *hannya* (wisdom).

Hannya is a transliteration of the Sanskrit word *prajna*, which is colloquially called *panya*. This wisdom is acquired as a result of pursuing the precepts and meditation.

Within this training in the Buddhist path, the three learnings—precepts, meditation, wisdom—are "the three essential virtues" and consequently one third is seated meditation. The various Japanese terms *zen, zenjō, jō, zazen* all have exactly the same meaning.

The Ch'an (Zen) sect, founded before the sixth century in China, takes Bodhidharma (Daruma) as its founder. Bodhidharma was a priest who came to China from India. There is some doubt, however, as to whether he actually existed. If he did indeed exist, then he was a semi-legendary figure.

Within the Zen sect, which takes Bodhidharma as its founder, one directly grasps the heart of Buddha through seated meditation and to actually grasp the heart of Buddha one does seated meditation. Consequently, Zen is also called *Busshinshū,* "the Buddha heart sect."

Within Zen Buddhism, seated meditation is not one of the three teachings of precepts, meditation and wisdom. Seated meditation is not just one of the three. Rather, the precepts and wisdom are to be found within seated meditation. Meditation is everything. Therefore it is said to be a whole, one out of one.

This is the Zen way of thinking.

■ ■ ■

Eisai was born the child of a priest of Kibitsu Shrine in present-day Okayama City. He took the tonsure at Hiei-san and became a priest of the Tendai sect. Among the events of his life that deserve special mention is the fact that he was able to visit Sung

CHAPTER 4 KAMAKURA PERIOD 127

ていることです（1168年に5ヵ月間と1187年から91年までの5年間）。そして中国から禅宗を持ち帰り、日本で臨済宗を開きました。

けれども、栄西の思想は、どちらかといえば天台宗の考え方で、完全な一分の一の禅ではありません。むしろ三分の一の禅といったほうがよさそうです。

また、栄西は天台宗から京都においての布教を禁じられ、そのため活動の拠点を鎌倉に移し、幕府の庇護の下で臨済宗を広めました。臨済宗の中にあっても、そのような栄西の布教態度を嫌う人も少なくないようです。

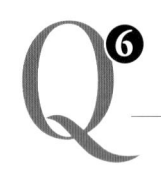

栄西

Q❻ 道元が中国から伝えた曹洞宗と臨済宗との違いを教えてください。

道元（1200-53）もまた比叡山で出家した天台宗の僧です。そして中国に渡り、如浄という師について禅を学び、真の悟りに達しました。道元と栄西との違いは、栄西が天台宗的な三分の一の禅を学んだのに対して、道元は一分の一の禅を学んだことです。

如浄の下で大悟した道元は、1227年に帰国しました。帰国後しばらくのあいだは、栄西が建立した京都の建仁寺に滞在しますが、1233年に洛南の深草に興聖寺を開創し、そこで布教を始めました。けれども、道元の場合もやはり比叡山からの迫害があり、道元は1243年に越前（福井県）に移り住みま

China twice (for five months in 1168 and for five years between 1187 and 1191). He brought Zen teachings back from China and founded Japan's Rinzai sect.

However, Eisai's thought was basically that of the Tendai sect and never completely reached the state of full "one out of one" Zen. Rather as far as he was concerned, Zen meditation was one of the three paths.

Further, the Tendai sect prohibited Eisai from proselytizing in Kyōto, so in order to promote Zen, he moved his base to Kamakura, where under the patronage of the shogunate he was able to spread Rinzai teachings. Still, within the Rinzai sect, there were no small numbers of people who disliked his attitude toward propagating.

❝ What is the difference between the Sōtō teachings and the teachings of the Rinzai sect?

Dōgen was also a Tendai priest who had studied at Mt. Hiei. He traveled to China where he studied Ch'an (Zen) teachings under Ju-ching and attained enlightenment. The difference between Dōgen and Eisai is that while Eisai studied a more Pure Land form of Buddhism, in which meditation was "one of three" elements, Dōgen learned the form in which meditation (zen) was the highest and best practice, or "one out of one."

After achieving his great enlightenment under Ju-ching, Dōgen returned to Japan in 1227. After his return, he resided temporarily at Kenninji, but in 1233 he established Kōshōji in Fukakusa in southern Kyōto, where he began proselytizing. Dōgen, too, came under persecution from the priests on Mt. Hiei, and in 1243 he moved to Echizen (present-day Fukui

す。その地に建立した大仏寺が、のちに永平寺と改称され、曹洞宗の拠点になりました。道元の入滅の地は京都ですが、その1ヵ月少し前までは彼は永平寺に居住していたのです。

さて、道元の思想ですが、それは、

——修証一等——

という言葉に要約できるでしょう。"修"とは「修行」であり、"証"は「悟り」です。修行と悟りが別個のものではなく、二つが同じものだというのが道元の主張です。

わたしたちは悟りを得るために修行をします。普通はそう考えられていますが、そのように考えると、悟りが目的になり修行は手段になってしまいます。そして、目的のためには手段を選ばず、といった誤った考え方にもなります。たとえば、大学に合格するために受験勉強をするようなものです。そうすると受験勉強がつまらないものになり、極端な場合はカンニングでもしたくなります。

そんな考え方はよくない、というのが道元の主張です。禅の修行は目的のための手段ではないのです。坐禅をすることそのものが目的でなければなりません。受験勉強について言えば、大学に入学したいのは勉強するためですね。楽しく勉強するために大学に行くのに、そのための勉強（受験勉強）が楽しくない、いやなものだというのは、本末転倒もはなはだしいですね。したがってわたしたちは、勉強することそのものを目的にすべきです。つまり、坐禅そのものが目的にならねばならないのです。それが道元の考え方です。

道元

prefecture). There he founded Daibutsuji, later renamed Eiheiji, which became the focal point of the Sōtō sect. Dōgen passed away in Kyōto, but he lived until the month before his death at Eiheiji.

Dōgen's thought can be distilled in the expression *shu shō ittō*. The character *shu* refers to ascetic practices, while *shō* refers to spiritual awakening. That is, "ascetic practice" and "enlightenment" are not separate, but are one and the same.

One would normally think that a person does ascetic practices in order to attain enlightenment, but in that way of thinking, enlightenment becomes a goal and ascetic practices are a means to that goal. That allows the mistaken view that we cannot select the method to achieve the goal. For example, it is like studying in preparation for passing an exam to enter a university. Thinking of it that way, the preparatory studying becomes boring, and in an extreme case, one might even want to cheat on the exam.

Such thinking is undesirable according to Dōgen. The practice of Zen is not a method of achieving a goal. The goal must be sitting in meditation itself. In terms of studying for an entrance exam, it is studying because you want to enter a university. Despite the fact that you are going to university in order to enjoy studying, in order to get there you are studying for the entrance exam and not enjoying it at all. It is a terrible case of mistaking the means for the end, of putting the cart before the horse. That is, seated meditation itself must be made the purpose. That is Dōgen's way of thinking.

それゆえ道元は、「只管打坐」ということを言っています。"只管"は宋代以後の口語で、「ひたすらに」の意味です。ただひたすらに坐禅せよ、というのが道元の主張でありました。

■■■

臨済宗の禅と曹洞宗の禅の違いは、前者が看話禅（公案禅ともいいます）、後者が黙照禅である点です。じつは"看話禅""黙照禅"といった言葉は、お互いが相手の禅風を批判して投げ掛けた言葉だったのですが、今日ではそれぞれが自己の禅風を誇って言う言葉になっています。

看話禅というのは、公案禅とも言われているように、禅の修行者が公案を使って悟りに達しようとするものです。公案というのは、禅の試験問題だと思えばいいでしょう。修行者は師から出された公案を一つ一つ解きながら、自己を磨くのです。

それに対して黙照禅は、公案を使わずに黙々と坐禅するのが特色です。その黙（坐禅）の中に照（慧）があると考えられています。道元の考え方は、この黙照禅の考え方にもとづいています。

Q❼ 鎌倉時代には、中国から多くの禅僧が日本に来ているようですが……。

その通りです。まず、1246年に執権北条時頼の招きで蘭渓道隆（1213–78）が来日しました。この1246年は、道元が越前に建立した大仏寺を永平寺と改称した年です。

Consequently, Dōgen uses the expression *shikan taza*, "just sitting in meditation." The term *shikan* has been used since the Sung dynasty as a colloquial expression meaning "single-mindedly" or "simply." Dōgen asserts that one should simply sit in meditation.

■ ■ ■

The difference between Rinzai and Sōtō is that the former is *Kanna* Zen or *kōan* Zen and the latter is *Mokushō* Zen. Actually these two terms were hurled (投げつける) as forms of criticism at the counterpart's form of Zen, but nowadays the terms are proudly used by the respective sects to describe their own style.

Kanna Zen, also called *kōan* Zen, is the form in which Zen practitioners use *kōan* in order to reach enlightenment. A *kōan* can be thought of as a Zen test question. The practitioner tries to work out one by one the *kōan* provided by his master and as he does so, he cultivates himself.

In contrast, *Mokushō* Zen is characterized by silently sitting in meditation, without employing *kōan*. It is believed that *shō* (light > wisdom) comes from *moku* (silence > seated meditation). Dōgen's way of thinking is based on this belief in achieving wisdom through silent contemplation (瞑想).

66 In the Kamakura period, a number of Chinese Zen priests came to Japan, didn't they?

That is true. First, in 1246, upon the invitation of the regent Hōjō Tokiyori, Lan-ch'i Tao-lung (Rankei Dōryū, 1213–78) came to Japan. This was the same year that Dōgen changed the name of Daibutsuji, in Echizen, to Eiheiji.

時頼は蘭渓を開山として鎌倉に建長寺を建立しました。そして蘭渓は大覚禅師と諡を受けています。これがわが国における最初の禅師号になります。

　蘭渓に続いて、1260年に兀庵普寧（1197-1276）が、1269年には大休正念（1215-89）が来日しています。
　そのあと、1279年に北条時宗に招かれて無学祖元（1226-86）が来日しました。彼は蘭渓入滅後の建長寺に入りましたが、また時宗が建立した円覚寺の開山となり、建長・円覚の両寺の住職を兼ねています。
　このほか、1299年には一山一寧（1247-1317）、1329年には明極楚俊（1262-1336）の来日がありました。

Q❽ では、次は日蓮ですね。日蓮は戦闘的な仏教者のように思われていますが、実際にそうだったのですか？

　日蓮（1222-82）は39歳のときに、『立正安国論』を書いて当時の実力者である前執権の北条時頼に献じました。『立正安国論』は正法（正しい教え）を立てることによって国の安泰が得られることを主張した書で、日蓮において「正法」とは『法華経』の教えにほかなりません。つまり、日蓮は、日本の仏教者のすべてが『法華経』の教えを重んじ『法華経』の精神に戻らねばならないことを主張したのです。具体的には、

日蓮

Tokiyori had him open Kenchōji in Kamakura. When Lan-ch'i died, he was given the posthumous name Daikaku Zenji (Zen Master Daikaku). This was the first time in Japan, that a priest was granted the title Zenji.

Following Lan-ch'i, Wu-an P'u-ning (Gottan Funei, 1197–1276) arrived in 1260, and Ta-hsiu Cheng-nien (Daikyū Shōnen, 1215–89) arrived in 1269.

Later, in 1279, at the invitation of Hōjō Tokimune, Wu-hsueh Tsu-yuan (Mugaku Sogen, 1226–86) arrived in Japan. Following the passing of Lan-ch'i, he entered Kenchōji and when Tokimune founded Engakuji, he served concurrently as abbot of both Kenchōji and Engakuji.

In addition, I-shan I-ning (Issan Ichinei, 1247–1317) arrived in Japan in 1299 and Ming-chi Ch'u-chun (Minki Soshun, 1262–1336) arrived in 1329.

> **Well then, next is Nichiren. He is thought to have been a militant Buddhist, but is that really true?**

When he was 39, Nichiren (1222–82) presented to the powerful former-regent Hōjō Tokiyori his "Treatise on Pacifying the State by Establishing Orthodoxy" (*Risshō Ankoku Ron*). This treatise insisted that by establishing the true, orthodox teachings of Buddha, the security of the country would be ensured, and of course by "true teachings" he meant the Lotus Sutra. In other words, Nichiren asserted that all the Buddhists of Japan should put high value on teachings of the Lotus Sutra and return to its spirit. In concrete terms, this meant manifesting the orthodox teachings by prohibiting Hōnen's *nenbutsu* Buddhism

当時の仏教界を席捲していた法然の念仏仏教を禁止することによって「立正」が実現し、「安国」が得られるといった主張になります。

けれども、政治権力はこのような日蓮の進言を聞きいれようとはしません。聞きいれないどころか、逆に日蓮に弾圧が加えられます。彼は40歳のときに伊豆に流罪になり、50歳のときには佐渡に流罪になりました。

ただ、日蓮の流罪をどう見るかに関しては、いささか問題があります。日蓮の側からすれば、これは「迫害」であり「弾圧」であり「法難」であるということになりますが、果たしてこれを「法難」と言えるでしょうか。鎌倉幕府は、日蓮の仏教教理の解釈が異端であり邪説であるから彼を処罰したのではありません。ただ日蓮が他宗を非難攻撃したことに対して、それが社会の秩序を乱し、安寧を紊乱させるということで彼を流罪にしたのです。その点では、日蓮の流罪は法然・親鸞の流罪とはまったく異質なものでした。

さて、日蓮は50歳で佐渡に流罪になりましたが、その佐渡の地において彼の思想は大きく転換をしました。じつは、日蓮宗の学者のなかには、彼の思想の転換を認めない人もいますが、わたしは「佐前」(佐渡流罪以前)と「佐後」(佐渡流罪以後)では、日蓮の思想・主張は大きく変わっていると思っています。

まず、「佐前」にあっては、日蓮は「天台沙門」(天台宗の僧)を名乗っていました。しかし「佐後」になると、彼は「本朝沙門」(日本の僧)を名乗ります。読者は思い出してください。天台宗は律令国家の仏教であって、天台宗の僧の役目は国家の安泰

which had swept across the contemporary world of Buddhism in Japan and thereby attaining a secure country.

However, the political authorities turned a deaf ear to Nichiren's counsel. Not only did they not take his advice, to the contrary they subjected him to pressure. At the age of 40, he was exiled to Izu, and at 50, he was exiled to Sado Island.

Some questions remain as to how one should view Nichiren's banishment. From Nichiren's side, this was oppression, suppression and religious persecution, but is it really appropriate to call it religious persecution? The Kamakura shogunate did not punish Nichiren because his interpretation of Buddhist creed was heretical or heterodox. He was exiled because his criticism of and attacks on other sects of Buddhism disturbed public order and threw public security into confusion. In this respect, Nichiren's exile was of an entirely different nature from that of Hōnen and Shinran.

Nichiren was 50 when he was exiled to Sado, and during his time there, his thinking underwent a drastic change. Actually, among scholars of the Nichiren sect, there are some who do not acknowledge that there was any such shift in his thinking, but I believe there was a major shift in his thinking and assertions between the period previous to his Sado exile and the period following it.

First of all, in the pre-Sado period, Nichiren identified himself as a "priest of the Tendai sect," whereas in the post-Sado period, as the reader will recall, he identified himself as a "priest of Japan." The Tendai sect is the Buddhism of the *ritsuryō* state, and the role of the monks of the Tendai sect was to pray for

を祈ることです。「佐前」の日蓮はまさにその国家の安泰を願って『立正安国論』を執筆しました。しかし、「佐後」の日蓮は、国家の安泰よりも日本の庶民の幸福を願っています。それが「本朝沙門」の名乗りになっています。ここに大きな思想の変化、というより発展があるのではないでしょうか。

　また、日蓮の思想の核心は、
　　――「南無妙法蓮華経」の御題目――
にあります。「妙法蓮華経」というのは『法華経』です。彼は『法華経』の教えに帰依し、『法華経』の教えを絶対とする立場をとったのです。
　ところが、「佐前」に執筆された『立正安国論』においては、『法華経』にはあまり言及されていません。そこで引用されている経典は、『金光明経』や『仁王経』などの、いわゆる「護国の経典」と呼ばれているものです。
　これは、『法華経』はあまり国家というものに関心を示していないからです。もともと仏教は「出世間の教え」であって、世間の中での成功・不成功といったものにとらわれることなく、世間を離れて、真の人間としての生き方を教えています。その基本的な態度は大乗仏教にも継承されています。だから初期の大乗仏教の経典である『法華経』は、国家や政治に関心を持たないのです。
　けれども、インドにおいても後世になると国家権力が強大になり、仏教教団も国家権力の庇護を受けなければ存続できなくなり、そうなってからつくられた経典には「護国」といった思想が見られます。日蓮はそれらの経典によって、「護国」すなわち「立正安国」の思想を展開したのです。それが「佐

the security of the country. As a priest, Nichiren without doubt composed his *Risshō Ankoku Ron* out of a desire for peace and security of the state. However, post-Sado Nichiren was praying for the happiness of the common people of Japan, rather than the security of the state. That is what is behind his calling himself "a priest of Japan." It is a major change in thinking, or more accurately, a major step forward.

The core of Nichiren's thought is the reciting of the title of the Lotus Sutra: *Namu myōhō renge-kyō* (Take refuge in the Sutra of the Lotus Flower of the Wonderful Law). "*Myōhō renge-kyō*" is the Lotus Sutra. He believed in the Lotus Sutra and believed its teachings to be absolute.

However, in the *Risshō Ankoku Ron*, which he wrote before going into exile on Sado, he does not make much reference to the Lotus Sutra. Instead, he refers to the *Konkōmyō-kyō* (The Golden Splendor Sutra) and the *Ninnō-gyō*, sutras that one could call scriptures for protecting the nation.

This is because the Lotus Sutra does not show much interest in the nation. Originally, Buddhism is "teaching for leaving the world." It is not concerned with success or lack of success, but rather teaches how one, separated from the world, should live as a true human being. That fundamental attitude is carried on in the Mahayana tradition. Therefore the Lotus Sutra, an early Mahayana scripture, maintains no interest in either the nation or politics.

However, in the later periods in India, the state grew more powerful, and the Buddhist organizations could not continue to exist without the patronage of the power of the state, and once that happened, the idea of "protecting the nation" began to appear. Through such sutras, Nichiren developed the thinking of *Risshō Ankoku*, manifesting orthodox teachings and protecting

前」の時代の代表作である『立正安国論』です。

　だが、「佐後」においては、日蓮は『法華経』だけを重んじています。明らかに日蓮の思想は変わっているのです。わたしはそう思います。
　それゆえ、戦闘的仏教者としての日蓮のイメージは「佐前」のそれです。「佐後」の日蓮には、弟子たちや信者たちに対する深い思いやりが見られます。わたしは、日蓮はやさしさにあふれた仏教者だと思っています。

Q❾ もう一つ、時宗が残っていますね。

　時宗の開祖は一遍（1239–89）です。彼は、『阿弥陀経』の中に、「南無阿弥陀仏」の念仏を称えた者には、その人の臨終の際に阿弥陀仏が出現してくださると説かれていることにもとづいて、日常生活のあらゆる瞬間を臨終の時と考えて念仏するようにと教えました。一遍は自分の寺も持たず、日本全国を遊行して念仏の教えを広めました。それゆえ、時宗は遊行宗とも呼ばれます。

一遍

Q❿ 鎌倉時代には多くの新仏教が誕生しました。そうすると、旧仏教は滅びてしまったのですか？

　たしかに新仏教の成立はわれわれの目を引きます。けれども、それらの宗派が民衆のあいだにどれ

140　第4章　鎌倉時代

the nation. This is the thinking that is represented in his "pre-Sado" treatise *Risshō Ankoku Ron*.

After Sado, however, Nichiren stresses only the Lotus Sutra. It seems clear to me that Nichiren's thought changed.

Therefore, Nichiren's image as a militant Buddhist comes from the pre-Sado period. Post-Sado, Nichiren's thought shows a deep consideration for his disciples and believers. It is my belief that Nichiren is a Buddhist who is filled with tenderness.

66 And then there is the Ji sect, right?

The founder of the Ji sect was Ippen (1239–89). Based on the *Amida-kyō* teachings, Ippen preached that to anyone who recited the *nenbutsu* "*Namu Amida Butsu*," Amida would appear at the end of that person's life, and therefore one ought to constantly, through daily life devote oneself to invoking Amida. Ippen did not have his own temple but rather traveled about the entire country, spreading the teaching of *nenbutsu*. As a result, the Ji sect is called the "proselytizing journey" sect.

66 Many new forms of Buddhism appeared in the Kamakura period. Did the older forms cease to exist?

To be sure, the organization of new forms of Buddhism attracts our attention, but when we consider just how deeply these sects

だけ浸透したかといえば、いささか疑問が残ります。法然や一遍の念仏運動は民衆のあいだに広まっていますが、親鸞は越後に流罪になったあと、赦免になっても京都に帰らず関東に行きました。そこで数百人の信者に囲まれて生活していましたから、影響といってもその程度です。道元も越前の永平寺で暮らしていますし、日蓮も最後は身延山に暮らしています。だから、新仏教が庶民のあいだで知られるようになるのは、ずっと後世になってからです。

むしろ鎌倉時代でわれわれが注目すべきは、叡尊（1201-90）と忍性（1217-1303）の２人でしょう。

叡尊は、西大寺を拠点に戒律復興運動を推進した僧で、真言律宗の開祖です。彼は畿内ばかりでなく東国にまで持戒（戒を守ること）、とくに殺生禁断を説いて回り、名望を集めています。彼はまた、非人救済などの積極的な社会救済事業を推進しています。

忍性は叡尊の弟子です。彼もまた師の叡尊と同じく、貧しい人々の救済やハンセン病患者の救済にあたりました。また、聖徳太子を追慕して、病院や馬の病舎を設置したり、出版事業などさまざまな社会救済事業を推進しています。

Q⓫ 神道＝やまと教のほうには、何らかの動きがありましたか？

やまと教というのは、言うならば民衆神道です。それは日本人に日本人としての生き方を教えるもの

spread among the common people, a certain degree of doubt remains. The *nenbutsu* movement of Hōnen and Ippen spread among the people. But after being exiled to Echigo and subsequently pardoned, Shinran did not return to Kyōto but instead went to the Kantō region. He lived there surrounded by several hundred followers, but that was the extent of his influence. Dōgen lived at Eiheiji in Echizen, and Nichiren lived his last years on Mt. Minobu. Therefore, the newer Buddhism became known among the ordinary people in much later times.

Rather, we ought to direct our attention to Eizon (1201–90) and Ninshō (1217–1303).

Eizon is the priest who promoted the movement of observance of the precepts centering on Saidaiji and who founded the Ritsu school of Shingon. Not only in the Kinai region but even as far as the eastern provinces, Eizon built a reputation for preaching the observance of Buddhist precepts, especially against hunting and fishing. He also actively promoted social relief work among the *hinin*, the outcaste groups.

Ninshō was Eizon's disciple. Like his master, he took upon himself the provision of relief to the indigent and sufferers of Hansen disease. Cherishing the example of Prince Shōtoku, he also established hospitals and veterinarian infirmaries for horses, as well as promoting various social aid enterprises including publishing enterprises.

> **Were there activities in Shintoism, that is, Yamatoism?**

In terms of Yamatoism, if there is anything to comment on, it is popular Shintoism. It teaches the Japanese way of living to

です。教えるといっても、誰か神官が説教するわけではありません。長老・古老と呼ばれる人々が、いろんな機会にいろんな出来事を通じて「生き方の知恵」を教えます。そういうかたちでやまと教は伝承されるものです。

　ですから、やまと教には、いつの時代にあってもこれといった動きはありません。もちろん、日本人の生き方は、時代が違えば変わってきます。しかし、その変化は知らず知らずのうちに起きるものであって、誰かがイニシアティブ（主導権）を取って変わるものではないのです。ですから、その意味では「動き」はなかったと言うべきでしょう。

　ところで、そのような民衆の神道であるやまと教に対して、国家の神道があります。この国家の神道を"国家神道"と表記すれば、明治以後に神道の国教化政策の下でつくられた国家宗教とまちがえられますので、"国家の神道"と表記します。これは為政者(せいしゃ)のあいだで信奉されたイデオロギーにほかなりません。まあ、為政者も日本人ですから、その為政者に日本人らしい生き方を教えたという点では宗教的色彩もありますが、それは宗教というより政治イデオロギーと見たほうがよいでしょう。

　この国家の神道においては、鎌倉時代（1192–1333）に、『神道五部書(しんとうごぶしょ)』といった教典がつくられています。この教典は奈良時代にすでに成立していた書だと記されていますが、実際には鎌倉時代中期につくられた偽書(ぎしょ)であることが明らかになっています。では、なぜそのような偽書がつくられたかといえば、国家の神道の担い手たちはみずからの宗教に「教義」を与えることによって、仏教に対抗できる理論的武装をしたかったからです。

the Japanese people. Even though we use the word "teach," that does not mean that some priest goes around preaching. People known as "elders" or "old folks" teach "wisdom for living" on different occasions and at various events. It is through this method that Yamatoism is passed down to the next generation.

For that reason, regardless of the period, there is no specific development one can point to. Of course, the Japanese way of life changes as times change. However, those changes occur by imperceptible degrees, and they do not occur because someone took initiative. In that sense, one ought to say that there was no "activity."

In contrast with Yamatoism, folk Shintoism, there is national Shintō. If we refer to this national form as "State Shintō," then it may be confused with the national religion that was fostered under the Meiji government to use Shintō to further government policies, so here we should refer to it as simply "national Shintō" or "Shintō of the country." This is none other than the ideology espoused by those in the administration. These statesmen are Japanese, and in the sense that it taught these statesmen a Japanese way of living it did have a religious tinge, but it is best to see it as less of a religion and more of a political ideology.

Within this national form of Shintō, in the Kamakura period (1192–1333), the sacred writings called *Shintō Gobusho* were composed. It was recorded that these volumes of scriptures were already in existence in the Nara period, but it has been made clear that it was a forged volume actually created in the middle of the Kamakura period. The reason it was forged was to give "doctrine" to supporters of the national form of Shintō, in hopes of providing themselves with theoretical armament with which to oppose Buddhism.

けれども、民族宗教には本来は教義・理論はありませんから、『神道五部書』の内容は仏教や儒教・道教の教義の寄せ集めでしかありません。その意味では、われわれはこれを無視していいと思っています。

　けれども、国家の神道側のこのようなコンプレックスにもとづく動きが、明治になってつくられた国家神道の伏線になっていることを忘れてはならないでしょう。

However, folk religion essentially has neither doctrine nor theory, so the contents of this *Shintō Gobusho* are little more than a mixture of doctrines from Buddhism, Confucianism and Daoism. In that sense, I believe we can ignore this work.

However, we should not forget that this development based on the spiritual complex felt by the followers of national Shintō foreshadows the State Shintō created once the Meiji period arrived.
~の前兆となる

第5章　室町時代

キリスト教がやってきた

Q❶ 室町時代の仏教界の大スターといえば一休さんですね。

　室町時代に入る前の鎌倉末期に、禅宗寺院の格付けが行われていました。幕府と公家の氏寺である五ヵ寺（建長寺・円覚寺・寿福寺・浄智寺・浄妙寺）を選んで、「鎌倉五山」とするものです。その後、室町時代になって、夢窓疎石（1275–1351）とその門流の発展に伴って、「京都五山」が選定されました。「京都五山」は、南禅寺を五山の上位に置き、天竜寺・相国寺・建仁寺・東福寺・万寿寺でもって構成されます。

　ところで、夢窓疎石は、鎌倉時代に中国より来日した無学祖元の孫弟子にあたります。彼は室町幕府初代将軍の足利尊氏（1305–58）から帰依を受けたほか、7代の天皇から国師号を賜り、またその弟子1万3000余と言われるほどの、南北朝時代（1336–92）の仏教界の大スターでありました。

　さて、一休宗純（1394–1481）ですが、夢窓が南北朝時代の仏教

一休

CHAPTER 5 MUROMACHI PERIOD

Christianity Arrives

66 Isn't Ikkyū the great star of the Buddhist world in the Muromachi period?

In the late Kamakura period, prior to the beginning of the Muromachi period, Zen temples were divided into ranks. The five temples supported financially by the bakufu and the aristocratic families—Kenchōji, Engakuji, Jufukuji, Jōchiji and Jōmyōji— were selected as the Kamakura Gozan. Later, in the Muromachi period, accompanying the development of the branch of the school of Musō Soseki (1275–1351), the Kyōto Gozan were selected. The Kyōto Gozan consisted of Nanzenji in the superior rank over Tenryūji, Shōkokuji, Kenninji, Tōfukuji and Manjuji.

Musō Soseki was a second-generation disciple of Mugaku Sogen, who came to Japan from China during the Kamakura period. In addition to gaining the patronage of Ashikaga Takauji (1305–58), the first Muromachi shōgun, he received from seven generations of emperors the title Most Reverend Priest (*Kokushi*), and was said to have gathered as many as 13,000 disciples, making him the greatest luminary of the Buddhist world of the Nanbokuchō period (1336–92).

If Musō Soseki was the brightest star of the Nanbokuchō period, then Ikkyū Sōjun (1394–1481) was his equivalent in

界の大スターであるのに対して、一休は室町時代 (1392-1573) の大スターです。と同時に、一休は夢窓の門流に対抗して動いている節があります。というのは、南北朝の時代には京都の大徳寺は花園上皇や後醍醐天皇の帰依を得て、五山の上に列せられたのですが、室町時代になると夢窓派の台頭によって大徳寺は格下げになりました。一休は、堺の豪商の援助によって、その大徳寺を再興させることに全力を尽くしています。

　一休は、どうやら後小松天皇の落胤のようです。いま、一休の墓は宮内庁が管理しています。しかし、そのような出自にもかかわらず（あるいは、そのような出自のゆえに、と言うべきかもしれませんが）、一休は庶民にまじって自由奔放に生きています。ともかく彼は、僧侶が権力にへつらい、おもねることを嫌ったのです。それゆえ彼は「風狂の禅者」と呼ばれています。"風狂"とは、常軌を逸した人をいいます。

　なお、一休を主人公にしたさまざまな「一休頓智咄」がありますが、その大部分は江戸時代になってからつくられた創作話です。

Q❷ 本願寺教団の蓮如も、また室町時代の僧として有名ですね。

　蓮如 (1415-99) は本願寺7世存如の長男です。本願寺というのは、本来は寺ではなしに、浄土真宗の開祖である親鸞の遺骨を改葬し影像を安置した廟堂でありました。その廟堂を、親鸞の曾孫の覚如が寺院化して「本願寺」と号したのです。覚如は親鸞

the Muromachi period (1392–1573). One view holds that Ikkyū opposed Musō's branch. That is to say, during the Nanbokuchō period, Daitokuji in Kyōto obtained the support of Emperor Hanazono and Emperor Godaigo and was ranked above the Gozan temples. But when the Muromachi period arrived, through the influence of the Musō group, Daitokuji was demoted. With the support of the wealthy merchants of Sakai, Ikkyū devoted all of his energies to reviving Daitokuji's fortunes.

It would appear that Ikkyū was the illegitimate son of Emperor Gokomatsu. Ikkyū's tomb is currently maintained by the Imperial Household Agency. However, despite such family connections (or perhaps one should say because of them), Ikkyū led a free-spirited life mingling with the common people. At any rate, he disliked the fact that priests played up to and curried favor with the authorities. He was often described as a practitioner of an unconventional "mad Zen." Fūkyō, the phrase used to describe him, means a person who is eccentric.

Further, there are a number of comic stories with Ikkyū as their protagonist, but most of them are fictional tales that were created in the Edo period.

66 Rennyo of the Honganji is another well-known priest of the Muromachi, isn't he?

Rennyo (1415–99) was the eldest son of Zonnyo, 7th-generation head abbot of the Honganji. Honganji was originally not a temple but a mausoleum where the remains of the Jōdo Shin sect founder Shinran and his image were enshrined. Shinran's great-grandson Kakunyo converted the mausoleum into a temple

を「本願寺聖人」と称し、みずからを第3世に位置づけたのです。蓮如は、その本願寺の第8世にあたります。

　43歳で第8世となった蓮如はさまざまな改革を行いましたが、これが比叡山衆徒の反発を買い、京都大谷にあった本願寺は破壊されます。しかし蓮如は、1471年に越前（福井県）の吉崎の地に坊舎（吉崎御坊）を建立し、ここを拠点に布教活動を展開しました。

　蓮如の布教方法は、「御文」（「御文章」ともいいます）と呼ばれる手紙を信者に送り、この手紙を通して親鸞の教えを平易に説くことでした。その活発な教化活動は北陸から東海・東国・奥州にまで及びました。蓮如を慕う門徒は農民が中心でしたが、この門徒の集まりは勢力を増し、ついに在地領主と対立するようになります。そこで蓮如は抗争を避けるべく、1475年には吉崎を離れます。そしてそのあとは摂津・河内・和泉で布教活動を続けました。

　なお、蓮如は、生涯5人の妻と結婚し（いずれも前妻の死後に後妻を迎えています）、13男14女をもうけています。嫡出子（正妻から出生した子）の数としては、ひょっとすればこれはギネス・ブックものかもしれませんね。

蓮如

Q❸ 浄土真宗の盛んな土地で一向一揆が起きたのですね。どうしてですか……？

　蓮如の布教によって、浄土真宗の本願寺派は大勢の信者を獲得しました。彼らは農民が中心ですが、

and named it Honganji. Kakunyo called Shinran "Honganji Shōnin" and considered himself to be the 3rd-generation Patriarch. Rennyo was the 8th Patriarch of Honganji.

Upon becoming the 8th-generation Patriarch at the age of 43, Rennyo carried out a variety of reforms, but that provoked a backlash from the warrior-priests on Mt. Hiei, and Honganji, which was located in the Ōtani area of Kyōto, was destroyed. However, Rennyo erected monks' quarters at Yoshizaki in Echizen (present-day Fukui prefecture) in 1471, and from this base expanded efforts in propagation.

Rennyo's propagation method was the sending of epistles, called *ofumi*, to his followers, explaining in plain language the teachings of Shinran. This active evangelizing activity reached from Hokuriku to as far away as the Tōkai, Kantō and Ōshū regions. The adherents who followed Rennyo were mainly farming people, and as the gatherings of these believers grew in influence, they came into conflict with the feudal lords of the lands where they resided. Therefore, in order to avoid conflict, in 1475 Rennyo left Yoshizaki. From that time forward, he continued efforts at proselytizing in Settsu, Kawachi and Izumi.

During his lifetime, Rennyo married five times (each after the death of the previous wife), and had 13 sons and 14 daughters. The number of his legitimate children may well qualify him for the Guiness Book.

❝ Why is it that where the Jōdo Shin sect flourished there were also uprisings of Ikkō followers?

Through Rennyo's efforts in propagation, the Honganji branch of the Jōdo Shin sect acquired a large group of believers. They

そこに商工業者や武士などが加わっています。そして、さらには当時"一向衆"と呼ばれていた時宗の門徒が大勢加わりました。そこで、最初は"一向衆"あるいは"一向宗"は時宗の門徒を指す言葉であったのですが、戦国時代にはそれが浄土真宗の門徒を指す言葉になりました。この一向衆（一向宗）が領主権力に対して起こした一揆（武装蜂起、闘争）を一向一揆といいます。

考えてみれば、宗教教団が大量の信者を獲得して一つの社会勢力になれば、既存の勢力と衝突し、対立、拮抗するのは当然のことです。本願寺教団が量的拡大をとげると、領主権力ばかりでなく、他の宗教勢力からの圧迫が加わります。その圧迫に抵抗し、また本願寺教団の門徒自身の社会的・政治的な要求にもとづいて一揆が起きるのは歴史的必然です。

そして、その一揆が成功すれば、たとえば1488年に加賀国（石川県）でおきた一揆のように、約100年間にわたって本願寺門徒が加賀国を実質支配することもありました。また、のちには本願寺教団そのものが一つの武装勢力となり、戦国動乱の中で戦国諸大名と対立抗争するようになります。しかし、最終的には、本願寺勢力は織田信長（1534-82）によって撃破され、一向一揆は幕を閉じます。逆に言えば、織田信長は一向一揆を潰すことによって、畿内諸国の統一を実現したのです。

were largely farmers, but they included merchants, craftsmen and warriors. They also included large numbers of Ji sect followers who were at that time called the "*Ikkō shū.*" In the beginning, *Ikkō shū* was a term referring to adherents of the Ji sect, but during the Sengoku period (Period of Warring States), the term came to mean members of the Jōdo Shin sect. The armed uprisings the members of the *Ikkō shū* led against the authority of the feudal lords are known as *Ikkō ikki*, uprisings of Ikkō sect followers.

When one thinks about it, it is only a matter of course that when a religious organization acquires a large number of followers and becomes a social force it conflicts with, opposes and stands against the existing power structure. When the Honganji organization achieved a quantitative expansion, it came under pressure from not only feudal authorities but also from other religious powers. It was historically inevitable that uprisings would occur based on the resistance to such pressures and on the social and political demands of the believers of the Honganji organization.

When such an uprising succeeded, as it did in the uprising of 1488 in Kaga domain (present-day Ishikawa prefecture), the result was de facto control of Kaga by the Honganji followers that lasted for approximately a century. Subsequently, the Honganji adherents themselves became an armed group and during the upheavals of the Sengoku period, they engaged in armed conflict with various feudal lords. However, Honganji forces were ultimately crushed by Oda Nobunaga (1534–82), and the *Ikkō ikki* uprisings came to an end. Conversely, it can be said that as a result of crushing the *Ikkō ikki*, Oda Nobunaga was able to bring about the unification of the various provinces within the Kinai region.

Q❹ キリスト教は日本に、いつ、どのようにして伝わって来たのですか？

1549年の夏、イエズス会のフランシスコ・ザビエル（1506-52）が鹿児島に上陸し、キリシタン宗門の布教を始めたのが、キリスト教（カトリック）の日本への伝来の最初です。

布教当時は"南蛮宗""伴天連宗"などと呼ばれましたが、やがてポルトガル語を音写した"キリシタン"の呼称が一般的になり、"吉利支丹"の漢字が宛てられました。しかし、のちにはキリシタンが禁教になり、江戸時代の5代将軍徳川綱吉のとき以降は、"吉"の字を避けて"切支丹"と表記されるようになったのです。

ザビエル

なお"伴天連"は、ポルトガル語の"パードレ"（神父の意）の宛て字です。

ザビエルが属するイエズス会（"耶蘇会""ジェスイット会"ともいいます）は、当時、ヨーロッパでは宗教改革の勢力が強く、ローマ法王の権力が凋落の傾向にあったのを憂えたイグナティウス・デ・ロヨラ(1491-1556)が、学生たちに呼びかけてつくった信仰グループです。彼らは、法王への絶対服従と海外布教への献身を誓いあっていました。

このイエズス会士であったザビエルは、ローマ法王に選ばれて宣教のためにインドのゴアに来ました。そしてそこを拠点にして、マラッカ、モルッカ諸島へと足を伸ばし、キリスト教の宣教に活躍していました。

1547年夏、ザビエルはマラッカでアンジロー（ヤ

❝ How and when was Christianity transmitted to Japan?

In the summer of 1549, Francis Xavier (1506–52) of the Society of Jesus (also known as the Jesuits) landed at Kagoshima and began propagation of Christianity. This was the first introduction of Christianity (Catholicism) to Japan.

At the time of this propagation, the religion was called "the Nanban sect," "the Bateren sect" (after the Japanese word for Portuguese Jesuit priests) and other names, but before long the teachings came to be called *Kirishitan*, a transliteration of the Portuguese which was given the characters 吉利支丹 for phonetic reasons only. However, before long the new religion was banned, and following the fifth shōgun Tokugawa Tsunayoshi, whose name contained the character 吉, the name was altered to 切支丹.

For information's sake, the term 伴天連 (*bateren*) is the Japanese term for the Portuguese word *padre* meaning *priest*.

The Society of Jesus (in Japanese called *Yasokai* or *Jesuittokai*) to which Xavier belonged was a group founded by Ignatius de Loyola (1491–1556), who feared that under pressure from the strengthening forces of religious reformation (the Reformation) the power of the Pope was declining and issued a call to seminary students. They pledged to devote themselves to absolute obedience to the Pope and to the propagation of the faith overseas.

Xavier, a member of the Jesuits, was selected by the Pope to travel to Goa in India to perform missionary work. With Goa as his base, Xavier extended his proselytizing activities as far as Malacca and the Moluccas Islands.

In the summer of 1547, Xavier encountered a Japanese named

ジローとも伝えられます）という名の日本人に出会います。そしてこのアンジローを通して、高い文化を持った日本という国の存在を知り、日本への布教を決意しました。そして1549年に、アンジローの案内でザビエルは鹿児島にやって来たのです。

さて、ザビエルを迎えた鹿児島の領主の島津貴久（たかひさ）は、いちおう彼を歓迎しています。しかし、島津貴久の関心はキリスト教の教えではなく、ポルトガル船による南蛮貿易にありました。だが、ザビエルに布教を許したものの、その代償ともいうべきポルトガル船はいっこうにやってきません。そこで失望した島津貴久は、まるで厄介払い（やっかいばらい）をするかのごとくザビエルを京都に行かせます。

もっとも、ザビエルのほうは、天皇か将軍に会って、日本全土の布教の許可を得たいと思っていましたから、喜んで京都に行きました。

しかしながら、京都においてザビエルは冷たくあしらわれました。その理由は、彼が献上品を持って行かなかったからだとされています。またザビエルは、当時、仏教学のメッカともいうべき比叡山に登り、仏教僧と宗論をたたかわすことも考えたようですが、これも異国の僧の入山を拒む比叡山の掟があって実現しませんでした。

そんなわけでザビエルは長崎の平戸（ひらど）に行き、そこでたくさんの献上品を仕入れて、西国周防（すおう）（山口県）の領主である大内義隆に近づきます。そして、山口での布教を許され、また廃寺となっていた大道寺という寺を与えられ、これが日本最初のキリスト教の教会となりました。

Anjirō (also known as Yajirō) in Malacca. Through this Anjirō, Xavier learned of the existence of a country named Japan which possessed a high level of culture, and he made up his mind to propagate Christianity there. So it was that in 1549, with Anjirō as his guide, Xavier arrived in Kagoshima.

Shimazu Takahisa, the feudal lord of Kagoshima, tentatively[一時的に] welcomed Xavier. However, Takahisa's interest was not in the teachings of Christianity but rather in trade with the Iberian peninsula by means of Portuguese ships. In spite of that, while he permitted Xavier to propagate within his domain, the anticipated compensation[代償] was not to be had—not a single Portuguese ship came into his ports. The disillusioned Takahisa, as if to rid himself of a nuisance[厄介もの], had Xavier sent on to Kyōto.

Reasonably enough, Xavier happily went to Kyōto with hopes of meeting the emperor or the shōgun and obtaining permission to proselytize throughout all of Japan.

Contrary to his expectations, Xavier was treated coldly in Kyōto. It is held that the reason for this was that he went to Kyōto without gifts to present to the authorities. Furthermore, Xavier apparently thought he would climb Mt. Hiei, at the time the Mecca of Buddhist studies, and engage in doctrinal debates with the Buddhist priests. Due to the rules of Mt. Hiei, which forbade the entry of foreign priests to the mountain monastery, this desire too was left unfulfilled.

For that reason, Xavier went to Hirado in Nagasaki, stocked up on a large quantity of gifts and approached Ōuchi Yoshitaka, feudal lord of Suō (now in Yamaguchi prefecture) and protector of the lands to the west. Xavier was granted permission to proselytize in his domain and was given a deserted temple, Daidōji in Yamaguchi city which became the first Christian church in Japan.

Q5 その後、キリシタンは順調に伸びていったようですね。また、織田信長はキリシタンに好意的だったようですが……。

　おもしろいのは、フランシスコ・ザビエルの来日を、一般の人々は、
「天竺の坊主が新しい仏教の布教に日本にやって来た」
と受け取っていたことです。天竺はインドです。ザビエルはインドのゴアから日本に来たのですから、この認識はそれほどまちがってはいません。しかし、キリシタン（キリスト教）を仏教の新しい宗派と見る見方は、完全な誤りです。

　ザビエルによって始められたキリシタンの布教は、その後も多くの宣教師によって進められ、とくに西日本において多くの信者を獲得しました。ザビエルは2年と3ヵ月を日本に滞在したのですが、そのあいだに獲得した信者は約1000名。それが、1582年になると15万人になり、87年には20万人、教会数200になっています。布教は着実に進展したのですね。

　また、この布教活動にともなって、セミナリヨ（神学校）やコレジヨ（大学）が設立されてキリスト教教育が行われ、ローマ字によるキリスト教文学の翻訳や日本の古典文学、日本語辞書などの出版（キリシタン版といいます）も行われました。

　また、一方では、領内に教会を建て、布教に努力した大名たちもいます。彼らはキリシタン大名と呼ばれ、九州の大友宗麟、有馬晴信、大村純忠、近畿では高山右近や小西行長らが有名です。

> **It seems that Christianity spread smoothly after that. Was Oda Nobunaga also friendly toward Christianity?**

Interestingly enough, the general populace interpreted the arrival in Japan of Francis Xavier as the "arrival of a priest from *Tian-zhu* (an old Chinese term for India) who has come to propagate a new form of Buddhism." Because Xavier had arrived in Japan from Goa in India, that perception was not so farfetched. However, the view that *Kirishitan* (Christianity) was a new sect of Buddhism was entirely mistaken.

The propagation of Christianity begun by Xavier was later advanced by a large number of missionaries and they succeeded in winning many believers in western Japan. Xavier remained in Japan for two years and three months and during that time the missionaries secured about 1,000 converts. By 1582 that number increased to 150,000, and by 1587 there were 200,000 believers and 200 churches. Proselytizing progressed at a steady pace.

Accompanying this mission work, seminaries (seminario) and colleges (collegio) were established and Christian education was conducted. Christian literature was translated into Romanized Japanese and Japanese classic literature and Japanese dictionaries were published.

Churches were built within the feudal domains and some feudal lords made efforts to propagate the religion. These are called the "Christian daimyō," and among the well known are Ōtomo Sōrin, Arima Harunobu and Ōmura Sumitada of Kyūshū and Takayama Ukon and Konishi Yukinaga of the Kinki region.

織田信長（1534-82）の場合は、キリシタン大名たちとは少し事情が違います。信長はキリシタンを公認したのですが、それは彼が旧仏教勢力と対決し、抗争するためでした。つまり、仏教徒を牽制するためにキリシタンを利用したのです。

　ですから、次の豊臣秀吉（1536-98）の段階になって全国の平定が進むと、キリシタンを利用する必要はなくなります。それどころか、支配階級から見れば、宣教師を中心としたキリシタン信徒の精神的結合は、せっかく確立されようとしている封建的秩序にとって危険なものと映ります。それで秀吉も、その次の徳川家康（1542-1616）も、キリシタンを禁教にしたのです。

The case of Oda Nobunaga (1534–82) is somewhat different from that of the "Christian daimyō." Nobunaga gave official approval to the *Kirishitan*, but he did so to oppose and counter the older forces of Buddhism. In short, he employed the *Kirishitan* as a counterbalance to hold adherents of Buddhist groups in check.

As a result, at the next stage when Toyotomi Hideyoshi (1536–98) came along and the whole country was subjugated, it was no longer necessary to use the *Kirishitan*. Moreover, from the viewpoint of the ruling class, the spiritual bond between the *Kirishitan* believers, centered on the missionaries, appeared threatening to the feudal order that was just becoming established. For that reason, Hideyoshi—followed by Tokugawa Ieyasu (1542–1616)—banned Christianity.

第6章　江戸時代

仏教が骨抜きにされた

Q❶ まずキリシタン禁制について教えてください。

　前章の最後に言いましたように、全国統一を成し遂げた豊臣秀吉と徳川家康は、ともにキリスト教を敵性宗教とみなしてキリシタンの禁制に踏み切ります。

　彼らが目指していたのは集権的封建体制社会（幕藩体制社会）ですが、そのような社会においては、宗教が独自の力を持ってはならず、封建秩序に従順でなければなりません。

　やがて徳川幕府は仏教をうまく飼い馴らし、封建秩序に奉仕する番犬にしてしまいますが、外来宗教であるキリシタンは、そう簡単には番犬になりません。そこで彼らは、キリシタンを禁教にしたのです。

　まず秀吉は、1587年に伴天連追放令を発令しました。宣教師を国外に追放したのです。そして、長崎と畿内の主要な教会を破壊しました。もっとも、貿易は従来通り認めるという、大きな抜け穴は残していたのですが……。

　次に1596年、サン・フェリペ号事件が起きます。土佐に漂着したスペイン船サン・フェリペ号の

CHAPTER 6   EDO PERIOD

Buddhism Rendered Powerless

❝ First of all, why was Christianity banned?

As I said at the end of the previous chapter, Toyotomi Hideyoshi and Tokugawa Ieyasu, who accomplished the unification of the entire country, both took steps to ban Christianity, seeing it as a hostile religion.

They were both aiming at a centralized feudal society (the shogunate and domain system), and in such a society, religion could not be allowed to possess independent power. Instead it had to be made submissive to the feudal order.

In due course, the Tokugawa bakufu skillfully brought Buddhism under its control, making it a watchdog in the service of feudal order, but the imported Christianity was not so easily turned into a watchdog. For that reason, the leadership banned it.

First, in 1587 Hideyoshi issued an order expelling the foreign missionaries. This edict banished the missionaries from the country. Hideyoshi then had the main churches of Nagasaki and Kinai destroyed. Understandably, a major loophole was left which recognized foreign trade to continue as before.

Next, in 1596 the *San Felipe* Incident occurred, in which the Spanish ship by that name drifted ashore in Tosa and Hideyoshi

船荷を、秀吉が没収した事件です。この処置に抗議した航海長の発言や、ポルトガル人の讒言によって、秀吉はスペインが日本征服を計画していると疑いました。

　そして翌年、伴天連追放令を無視して布教をしていたフランシスコ会士6名と日本人信徒20名を捕らえ、これを長崎に送って処刑しました。これが26聖人の殉教と呼ばれるものです。

　さて、この事件をどう見ればよいでしょうか。なるほど、カトリック側から見れば、これは「殉教」でしょう。それゆえ、1862年にはローマ法王ピウス9世は、この26人を列聖しています。

　しかし、日本人からすれば、当時のカトリック教国のスペインに日本征服の意図がまったくなかったわけではなく、下手をすれば日本はインドのようにヨーロッパ諸国の植民地にされていたかもしれないのであり、その意味では豊臣秀吉の判断がむしろ正しかったと見るべきだと思います。

　その秀吉の判断は、次の家康にも受け継がれます。彼は1612年に「禁教令」を出し。翌年には「伴天連追放令」を発令しています。これによってキリシタン禁教は江戸幕府によって本格的に遂行されたのです。

Q❷ キリシタン禁教のために日本は鎖国をしたのですか？

　家康のキリシタン禁教の方針は2代将軍徳川秀忠 (1579-1632) に受け継がれます。彼は、1616年

confiscated its cargo. From the statements of the chief navigator of the ship and the false charges of the Portuguese, Hideyoshi came to suspect that the Spanish were plotting to conquer Japan.

The following year, six Franciscans and twenty Japanese followers were captured for ignoring the order expelling foreign missionaries and for propagating Christianity. They were sent to Nagasaki and executed. They are known as "the Twenty-six Martyrs of Japan."

How should we view this incident? As one would expect, the Catholics see this as martyrdom. As a result, in 1862 Pope Pius IX canonized the twenty-six.

However, from the Japanese perspective, Catholic Spain may well have intended to conquer Japan. If things had worked out poorly, Japan might have ended up as a colony of one of the European powers like India did. In that sense, I believe Hideyoshi's actions were justifiable.

Ieyasu followed Hideyoshi's assessment of the situation. In 1612 he issued the Ban on Christianity. The next year he issued the *Bateren tsuihō rei* (an edict expelling missionaries from the country). By these measures, the Edo bakufu eventually completed the complete banning of Christianity.

66 Was Japan completely closed to outsiders in order to ban the propagation of Christianity?

Ieyasu's policy of prohibiting the propagation of Christianity was taken over by the second shōgun, Tokugawa Hidetada

に、キリシタン禁制を百姓レベルにまで徹底するように命じ（それまではだいたいにおいて大名クラスに対する禁制でした）、またヨーロッパ船との貿易を長崎の平戸に限定しました。しかし、中国船との貿易は例外にされています。

ついで1633年、3代将軍徳川家光（1604–51）は、長崎奉行に将軍直参の旗本2名を任命し、この2名の者に老中から、
　——寛永鎖国令——
と呼ばれる指令が発せられました。もっとも、これはあとからつけた呼称であって、この文書に"鎖国"といった言葉が使われていたわけではありません。"鎖国"という言葉がはじめて文献に出てくるのは1801年です。

この年、長崎のオランダ通詞であった志筑忠雄が、1690年に来日したドイツ人医師のケンペルの著書『日本誌』を抄訳して、それを『鎖国論』と題したのが初見とされています。

それはともかく、「寛永鎖国令」は、のちに少しずつ改変され、最後に1639年に出された第5次鎖国令によって完成しました。それによると、

　1　日本人の海外往来禁止。
　2　キリシタンの禁止。
　3　対外貿易を長崎1港にのみ限定。

が定められています。これが実質的な「鎖国」でありました。

そしてこの「鎖国」は、1854年に、ペリー艦隊の来航の下で日米和親条約が調印されるまで、約200年間続きました。

(1579–1632). In 1616, Hidetada ordered the complete enforcement of the ban of Christianity down to the level of the peasantry, whereas until then the prohibition had generally applied only to the daimyō. Hidetada further restricted trade with European ships to Hirado in Nagasaki. Trade with Chinese ships, however, was exempted.

Subsequently in 1633 the third shōgun, Tokugawa Iemitsu (1604–51) appointed two direct retainers of the shōgun to serve as Nagasaki magistrates, and the senior councilor of the shogunate issued to these two officials directives called the *Kan'ei Sakokurei*, the edicts of seclusion. In fact, this term was only used later, and "*sakoku*" did not appear in these documents. The word *sakoku* (national seclusion) was not actually used until later, when it first appeared in records in 1801.

In that year, Shiduki Tadao, the Dutch interpreter at Nagasaki, is said to have used the term for the first time in *Sakokuron*, the title of his partial translation of the German physician Engelbert Kaempfer's "The History of Japan."

At any rate, the *Kan'ei Sakokurei* was amended a little at a time until the final edict was completed in 1639 with *Daigoji Sakokurei*, the fifth Sakoku edict. These edicts brought forth the following:

(1) Japanese were forbidden to travel overseas and then return.

(2) Christianity was banned.

(3) All external trade was restricted to one port at Nagasaki. To all intents and purposes, this was "national seclusion."

The policy of national seclusion continued for approximately two hundred years until the signing of the Japan-U.S. Amity Treaty upon the arrival of Commodore Perry's fleet in 1854.

Q❸ キリシタン禁教のために幕府がとった対策が、いわゆる「檀家制度」と呼ばれるものですね。

　江戸幕府はキリシタン禁教を徹底させるため、さまざまな方法でキリシタンの摘発を行いました。聖母マリア像やキリスト十字架像を足で踏ませて信者でないことを証明させる踏絵や、密告によって信者を摘発する制度などです。

　そして、キリシタンから転宗した者に対して、「寺請状」（「寺請証文」ともいいます）と呼ばれる証明書を寺僧に発行させます。結婚や旅行の際には、転宗者はこの寺請状を寺から受ける義務があります。

　この寺請状は、最初は転宗者のみに発行されていました（ただし、転宗者以外にも義務づけられた地方もあります）。ところが、1637年から翌年にかけて、天草と島原でキリシタンを中心とする百姓一揆が起きます。これを契機に厳格な宗門改めが行われ、1664年には、全国一律に寺請状と宗門改帳の作成が制度化されました。

　宗門改帳には、家ごとに檀那寺、戸主以下家族の名と年齢、妻の実家、嫁入りした年月日、雇い人の氏名と雇い入れの年月が記載されています。戸主はこれに判を押し、檀那寺、庄屋、五人組頭の証印を受けて宗門改役に提出するのです。

イエス・キリストの踏み絵

❝ Was the so-called danka system a measure that the bakufu took in order to ban Christianity?

In order to enforce the ban on Christianity thoroughly, the Edo bakufu took several measures to unmask Christian believers. The bakufu made plaques with images of either the Virgin Mary or the crucified Christ and forced suspected believers to tread on them to prove they were not Christians and used a system of exposing believers through betrayal.

For those who had converted from Christianity, it had Buddhist priests issue certification called *teraukejō (terauke-shōmon)* that verified that the person was affiliated with the priest's temple—to prove that the person in question was not a Christian. In order to marry and to travel, a convert was required to obtain such certification.

In the beginning this temple-issued certificate was issued only to those who converted (although in certain regions other categories of people were also required to have certification). However, from 1637 into the following year, an uprising of peasants occurred centering around Christians of Amakusa and Shimabara. Using this opportunity, a rigorous religious inquisition was carried out, and in 1664 a unified national certification and religious census register were institutionalized.

This religious census register recorded the family temple of each household, the names and ages of everyone in the household from the head downward, the parental household of the wife, the date of marriage, and the names of hired persons and when they began service. The household head affixed his seal, received the seals of the respective family temple, village headman and head of the five-household neighborhood unit and submitted it to the religious registry official.

これは、公権力による民衆の管理・統制にほかなりません。そして、この制度は、キリシタンがいなくなり、宗門改めの必要がなくなっても、ずっと温存・維持されました。
　このようにしてできたのが「檀家制度」です。全国民が寺請状を貰うために寺の檀家にならねばなりません。ただし、岡山藩や水戸藩では、寺請を廃して神社の請文にかえています。

　まあ、それは例外です。しかも、幕府の命によって離檀が禁じられていたもので、檀家のほうで寺や宗派の選択はできません。そのため寺院は檀家に対して、寺の伽藍の修復費や本山への寄付金の負担などを押し付けます。

　檀家がそれを断れば、宗門改帳から削られるので、断ることはできません。そうなると、寺院は宗教の施設ではなく、公権力の出先機関になってしまったわけです。ひどいものです。

Q❹ いま、本山への寄付金の負担と言われましたが、本山とはどういうものですか？

　江戸幕府は、寺院に檀家の管理を命じました。そうすると、こんどはその寺院のほうを幕府が管理せ

This was nothing less than control and regulation of the populace by government authorities. Further, even after Christians disappeared and religious inquisition was no longer deemed necessary, this system was left in place and remained in operation.

What evolved from this was the *danka* system, a system of patronage of Buddhist temples. Every family in the country was forced to become a supporter of a particular temple in order to receive necessary certification from that temple. In Okayama domain and Mito domain, however, temple certification was set aside and replaced with shrine certification.

That, however, was the exception that proved the rule. Moreover, by bakufu law, it was forbidden to withdraw from temple patronage, so parishioner households were allowed to select neither their own temple nor their sect of Buddhism. For that reason, the temples forced their respective supporting households to make donations for the repair of temple buildings and contribute to the head temple of the sect.

If a member household refused to do these things, it would be removed from the religion registry, so households were unable to refuse for whatever reason. That being the case, the temple ceased to be a religious facility and instead became a local agency of the central political authority. It was truly an outrage.

> **You have just mentioned the obligation to make donations to the head temples, but what exactly is a head temple?**

The Edo bakufu ordered Buddhist temples to supervise its parishioner households. By so doing, it then became necessary

ねばなりません。そのため、幕府は、各宗派の中心寺院を本山とし、その本山の下に末寺を統制させる「本末制度」を採用しました。もっとも、この本山・末寺の関係は、宗派ごとに中世には成立していたのですが、江戸時代になって幕府の手によりそれが法制化されたのです。

　この本末制度は、基本的にはピラミッド組織になっています。その標準的なピラミッド組織は、
　総本山―大本山―准大本山―別格本山―中本山
　―中本寺―小本寺―孫本寺―曾孫末寺―玄孫末寺
　といったものです。

Q❺ 寺院には寺格があったのですね。ではお坊さんには位がありましたか？

　仏教の本来からすれば、僧侶に位階というものはありません。釈迦はすべての出家者を平等に扱い、教団内においては出家年の前後だけを序列としました。すなわち、出家後の年数によって僧侶の序列がつけられたのです。

　ところが、日本において仏教は本質的に国家仏教であり、とくに古代における日本の僧侶は国家公務員でした。ですから当然のことながら、国家は僧侶に位階を与えてランクづけをし、僧位を定めました。したがって、このような僧位はすでに古代からあったもので、江戸時代になってからできたものではありません。

for the bakufu to supervise the temples. To do that, the bakufu introduced *hon-matsu seido*, a system of head and subordinate temples, which made the central temple of each sect the main temple (*honzan*) which was to exercise control over the subordinate or branch temples (*matsuji*). For that matter, the relationship of main and branch temples had been established within each sect during the medieval period, but at the hands of the bakufu that system was institutionalized during the Edo period.

The main temple-branch temple system is fundamentally a pyramid organization. The standard hierarchy is as follows:

[Translation is impossible and therefore omitted]

66 So each temple has a particular status in a hierarchy. Is the same true for the priests?

Properly speaking, within Buddhism priests do not have ranks. Shakyamuni 正確に treated all priests equally, and within the religious organizations the only hierarchy was based on the order in which the person renounced the world. In other words, the hierarchy of priests depended on the number of years that had passed after each person had become a priest.

However, in Japan, Buddhism became in essence state Buddhism, and particularly in ancient times, Japanese priests were national public servants. Therefore as a matter of course the state gave priests court ranks and determined their ranks within the priesthood. Consequently, priestly ranks were already in existence in ancient times and were not created for the first time during the Edo period.

Q❻ 「葬式仏教」という言葉がありますが、これは江戸時代に始まるものですか？

すでに述べたように、江戸幕府はキリシタン禁制のために、全国民が特定の寺院の檀家になることを義務づけました。それは、ある意味では、檀那寺（檀家の所属する寺）に戸籍を管理させたわけです。

そうすると、人が死ねば、檀那寺のほうではその死亡を確認する必要があります。宗門人別帳からその人の氏名を削るためです。そのために、檀那寺は檀家の葬式をやるようになったのです。

まあ、これは、寺にとって大きな収入になります。葬式だけではなしに、初七日や二七日、三七日、四七日、五七日、六七日、七七日（四十九日あるいは満中陰といいます）、そして百箇日、一周忌、三回忌（２年目に行われます）の追善法要を営むことによって、そのたびに僧侶は遺族から金を稼ぐことができるのです。おまけに、江戸時代の中ごろ以降になりますと、七回忌、十三回忌、十七回忌、二十三回忌、二十七回忌、三十三回忌の法要も義務づけられ、お寺はほくほくです。その結果、江戸時代の仏教寺院は、完全な「葬式産業」になってしまいました。

Q❼ 江戸時代以前は、誰がお葬式をしたのですか？

現代日本人の大半が、お葬式はお坊さんの仕事と思っていますが、それはとんでもない誤解です。冠

❝ Did what is called "funeral Buddhism" begin during the Edo period?

As was pointed out earlier, in order to ban Christianity, the Edo bakufu made it obligatory for everyone in the nation to became a "parishioner" of a specific temple. In a sense, the temple the household belonged to (*dannadera*) was given the responsibility for maintaining the household registries.

That being the case, when a person died, it was essential for the family's temple to confirm the death. This had to be done in order to remove the deceased's name from the religious census registry. For that reason, the family temple began to perform the funerals of its parishioner households.

This then became a major source of income for the temple. By performing ceremonies not only for the funeral, but also for the first seven days, the 2nd 7th day, 3rd 7th day, 4th 7th day, 5th 7th day, 6th 7th day, 7th 7th day (called *Shijūkunichi* or *Manchūin*), 100th day, the first anniversary, third anniversary (held during the second year), the priest was able to earn money from the surviving family on numerous occasions. On top of that, beginning from about the middle of the Tokugawa period, Buddhist memorial services were made obligatory for the 7th, 13th, 17th, 23rd, 27th and 33th anniversaries, which naturally pleased the temples. As a result, the Buddhist temples of the Edo period became complete "funeral enterprises."

❝ Who performed funerals before the Edo period?

The majority of Japanese today think that funeral ceremonies are a job for Buddhist priests, but that is a major misconception.

婚葬祭というのは習俗（社会的な風習）であって、基本的には宗教と無関係です。もっとも、葬式のほうはやや宗教に関係がありそうですが、宗教を否定していたかつての社会主義国でも、人が死ねば葬式をやります。

　また、最近の日本でも無宗教式の葬儀をする人もいることを思えば、葬式と仏教とはそれほど結びつくものでないことがお分かりいただけるでしょう。

　したがって、日本の現代仏教が「葬式仏教」と呼ばれていることは、仏教にとってとても恥ずかしいことです。
　では、お葬式は誰がするものでしょうか……？　じつは、いかなる国であれ、いかなる民族であれ、葬儀をする人は家の家長でした。家長が死ねば、後継者が葬儀をします。江戸時代以前の日本においても、葬儀をするのは各自が属する家の家長ないしは跡継ぎの役目です。

　ですから、江戸時代以前のお坊さんは葬儀にはタッチしていません。もっとも、天皇や貴族の葬儀には、僧侶が関与します。それから、僧侶が死ねば、僧は出家者であり、家を飛び出した人間ですから、その葬儀は家長はやってくれません。僧侶の葬式は、仲間であるお坊さんがするよりほかなかったのです。
　おもしろいことに、江戸時代になってお坊さんが檀家の葬式をやるようになったとき、その葬儀のスタイルはこの「仲間の葬式」でありました。それゆえ、死者にあわてて戒名をつけ、死者をお坊さんに

The ceremonies of coming of age, marriage, burial and other occasions are folkways (social manners and customs), and fundamentally these ceremonies have nothing to do with religion. True enough, funerals would seem to have some sort of connection with religion, but even in socialist nations which reject religion, a funeral is held when someone dies.

Furthermore, when you consider how even in Japan recently people are holding non-religious funeral ceremonies, I believe you will understand that funerals and Buddhism are not that closely bound together.

Accordingly, the fact that Buddhism in present-day Japan is referred to as "funeral Buddhism" is quite embarrassing for Buddhism.

Well then, who actually presides at a funeral? Whatever the country and whatever the ethnic group, the person who performs the funeral service is the head of the family. When the head of the family dies, the successor carries out the ceremony. In Japan prior to the Edo period, it was the duty of the head of each family or the heir and successor to perform the funeral rites.

That is why prior to the Edo period the Buddhist priest was not involved in the funeral rites. Priests were engaged in funerals of only the emperors and nobility. Also, when a priest died, because he had renounced the world and left his family, the head of his natural family would not perform the ceremony. It was left to his fellow priests to preside at his funeral.

Interestingly enough, when the priests began to perform funeral ceremonies for their parishioners during the Edo period, the funerals were in the style of "funerals for companions." Therefore the deceased would hastily be given a posthumous

します。戒名というのは、出家した者が師からつけてもらう僧名なのです。

また、こうして出家させた者に特訓を行います。お経を読んで聞かせ、仏教知識を授けるのです。お坊さんが読むお経は漢文で、さっぱり意味が分からないと文句を言う人がいますが、お坊さんは会葬者のためにお経を読んでいるのではありません。あれは死者に特訓を施しているのですから、会葬者に分からなくていいのです。まことにおかしな「葬式仏教」です。

Q❽ でも、江戸時代には良寛(りょうかん)といった有名な僧もいたのではありませんか……。

仏教寺院が堕落した。堕落したというより、宗教性を失って権力機構の末端を担うようになったのですが、かといって僧侶の全員が駄目になったのではありません。少数ではあっても、真の仏教僧としてまじめに生きていた僧侶もいました。そのうちの一人が、大愚良寛(たいぐ)(1758-1831)です。

良寛は越後（新潟県）の出身で、曹洞宗の禅僧です。しかし彼は宗門の人ではなく、その生涯を托鉢僧(たくはつそう)の生活に過ごしました。詩作と書道を楽しみ、子どもたちと遊ぶ清貧(せいひん)の生き方は、ある意味では仏教僧の原点に戻ったともいえるのではないでしょうか。

また、江戸時代の僧といえば、臨済宗

良寛

Buddhist name, thereby treating the deceased as a fellow priest. This *kaimyō*, posthumous Buddhist name, is the priestly name given by a master to a disciple who has renounced the world.

This master also conducts special training of the one who has become a priest. This master reads the sutras to the new "priest" and imparts to him knowledge of Buddhism. The sutra which the master recites is in classical Chinese, so some people complain that they cannot understand the meaning at all. But actually the attending priest is not reciting the sutra for the people attending the services. He is conducting special training for the deceased, so it is fine if the mourners do not understand anything at all. "Funeral Buddhism" is a really odd phenomenon.

❝ What about the famous priest named Ryōkan during the Edo period?

Buddhist temples degenerated. Perhaps degenerated is less accurate than saying the temples lost their religious nature and came to serve as the smallest unit of government administrative power. But still, that did not mean that all priests were incompetent. While they may have been few in number, some priests lived earnest lives as true priests of Buddhism. One of these was Daigu Ryōkan (1758–1831).

Ryōkan was born in Echigo province (present-day Niigata prefecture) and became a Zen priest of the Sōtō sect. He did not belong to a temple but rather spent his life as a mendicant monk. He enjoyed composing poetry, doing calligraphy, and playing with children in a lifestyle of honest poverty, which could be called a return to the starting point of the Buddhist priesthood.

Speaking of priests of the Edo period, we also find Hakuin

中興の祖と称される白隠慧鶴（1685-1768）もいます。彼は独自の公案体系を確立したことで有名です。

さらに盤珪永琢（1622-93）の名も加えるべきでしょう。盤珪もまた臨済宗の禅僧で、平話（日常の話し言葉）で禅を説いたので、一般民衆に仏教が理解されるようになりました。

それから、江戸初期に中国から来日した隠元隆琦（1592-1673）を開祖として、黄檗宗が開かれています。黄檗宗の本山は京都府宇治市の黄檗山万福寺です。

隠元

じつは、黄檗宗は、その教義や修行のやり方、儀礼も、臨済宗とほとんど変わりはありません。しかし、日本の臨済宗は鎌倉・室町時代に伝わり、早く日本化していました。遅れてやって来た隠元は、みずから中国禅の正統を誇示し、「臨済正宗」を名乗ります。また、歴代の住持も第16代までは中国僧がつとめ、仏像にしても建築にしても中国様式を維持したもので、臨済宗と異なる宗派になってしまいました。江戸時代の鎖国のうちにあって、万福寺は異国風の特異な寺でありました。

その隠元に師事した日本人の僧に鉄眼（1630-82）がいます。彼は仏教経典の集大成である「大蔵経」の刊行を決意し、全国を行脚して資金を集め、見事にそれを成し遂げました。刊行された「大蔵経」は「鉄眼版」あるいは「黄檗版」とも呼ばれています。その浄財を集めている途中で飢饉が起き

Ekaku (1685–1768) who is called the restorer of the Rinzai sect. He is known for establishing the unique scheme of the *kōan*, conundrums for Zen meditation.

We also ought to add Bankei Yōtaku (1622–93) to the list. Bankei was also a Zen priest of the Rinzai sect, and because he interpreted Zen teachings in plain, everyday language, the ordinary populace began to understand Buddhism more thoroughly.

Then at the beginning of the Edo period, Ingen Ryūki (Yinyuan Longji, Yin-yuan Lung-chi, 1592–1673) came from China to Japan, where he founded the Ōbaku sect. The main temple (*honzan*) of the Ōbaku sect is Ōbakusan Manpukuji in Uji city in Kyōto prefecture.

Actually, the Ōbaku sect, in terms of its doctrines, the practices it carries out and its observances, differs very little from the Rinzai sect. However, the Rinzai sect was transmitted in the Kamakura and Muromachi periods, and it was Japanized early on. Ingen, who arrived later, personally embodied the orthodoxy of Chinese Ch'an (Zen), identifying it as the orthodox Rinzai sect. In addition, Chinese priests had served as the head priest for 16 generations, the Buddhist images and architectural elements of the temple were continued in the Chinese style, so Ōbaku became a different sect from Rinzai. During the national seclusion of the Edo period, the Manpukuji was a uniquely foreign-style temple.

Among the Japanese priests who studied under Ingen was Tetsugen (1630–92). Tetsugen resolved to publish the *Daizōkyō*, the entirety of the Buddhist canon, and by making pilgrimages throughout the country in order to collect funds, he was able to accomplish this splendid task. This printing of the *Daizōkyō* is known as the Tetsugen or Ōbaku edition. During this period

たとき、彼はその浄財を難民のために放出し、再び募金を始めたのです。そのような美談が語り伝えられています。

江戸仏教は全体としては「葬式仏教」になってしまいましたが、良寛や白隠、鉄眼のような僧のいたことを、われわれは忘れてはならないでしょう。

Q❾ 江戸時代のやまと教はどうだったのですか……？

やまと教というのは民衆神道です。日本の庶民に日本人らしい生き方を教えるものが民衆神道です。

ところで、日本人の生活は、物質的な面では、古代から中世、中世から近世にかけてずいぶんと変化します。けれども、精神的な面から見れば、そこには大きな変化はなかったと思われます。外来宗教である仏教は、仏教のほうが日本化することに必死であり、日本人を仏教化しようとすることはほとんどなかったのです。

また、あとから入って来たキリスト教も、日本人を変える前に禁教になってしまいました。そういうことなので、やまと教は何の変化もなく江戸時代に存続しています。したがって、江戸時代のやまと教といったものを論ずる必要はなさそうです。つまり、日本の庶民は歴史の動きと関係なく、常に日本人らしい生活を続けていたことになります。

of collecting donations, a famine broke out. A commendable episode has been passed down which says that he passed out the donations he had collected for the printing to those people who were displaced by the famine, and then began once again to gather funds for the publication expenses.

Edo period Buddhism as a whole became "funeral Buddhism," but we should not forget that there were priests such as Ryōkan, Hakuin and Tetsugen.

❝ What was Yamatoism like during the Edo period?

Yamatoism is popular Shintō, one that teaches the Japanese way of life to the common people of Japan.

The Japanese way of life, in material terms, changed considerably over the period from ancient times, through the medieval period, to the modern era. However, when one looks at the spiritual aspects, it seems that there was no major change. Buddhism, which after all was a religion of foreign origin, strived desperately to become Japanized, making almost no effort to turn Japanese Buddhistic.

Even Christianity when it later arrived ended up being prohibited before it was able to change the Japanese people. As a consequence, Yamatoism continued without any change through the Edo period. Therefore, there would seem to be little need to comment on Yamatoism during the Edo period. That is to say, the common people of Japan continued to live in a Japanese way, unconnected with the movements of history.

第7章　近代

おかしな宗教が捏造(ねつぞう)された

Q❶ 明治になって、キリスト教は解禁されたのですね。

　じつは明治政府も、本当はキリスト教が嫌いでした。嫌いと言うより、キリスト教を危険視したのです。キリスト教化することによって、日本がヨーロッパ諸国の植民地にされることを恐れていたからです。

　したがって1868年（明治元年になります）には、明治政府は「キリシタン邪宗門(じゃしゅうもん)」の禁制を出し、翌年には長崎の浦上(うらかみ)で3400人以上のキリシタンを捕らえ、厳しい処分を加えました。

　このような動きに対してヨーロッパ列強は猛烈に抗議をします。それで明治政府は1871年には「宗門改」を廃止し、1873年には「キリシタン禁制」の高札を撤去し、浦上の信者たちを釈放しました。かくてようやくキリスト教は解禁になりました。

　しかし、表面的には解禁になったものの、政府のキリスト教に対する危険視は依然として続いていたことは忘れないでください。

CHAPTER 7   MODERN TIMES

Strange Religions are Concocted

66 The ban on Christianity was lifted in Meiji, right?

Actually, the Meiji government also disliked Christianity. Rather than simply disliking it, they regarded it as dangerous. The reason was that they were afraid that through Christian evangelism Japan might be turned into a colony of one of the various European nations.

Accordingly, in 1868 (the first year of the Meiji period), the Meiji government prohibited Christianity, and in 1869 more than 3,400 Christians in Urakami were jailed and harshly dealt with.

The great powers of Europe strongly protested this action. As a result, the Meiji government in 1871 ended "religious inquisition" (directed particularly against Christianity), and in 1873 removed the official notice boards announcing the ban on Christianity and released the Christians at Urakami. Thus the ban was finally lifted.

However, please remember that although superficially the prohibition was brought to an end, the government continued to see Christianity as dangerous.

Q❷ 「廃仏毀釈」とは何ですか？

　明治政府の基本方針は神道を国教にすることです。この場合の神道はやまと教ではなく、国家の神道です。いや、神道の国教化ではなしに、明治政府の目論見は新たに「国家神道」を創りあげることでした。

　ところが、われわれがこれまで見てきたように、長い歴史のあいだに神道と仏教は渾然一体となっていました。いわゆる神仏習合です。とくにやまと教において、その傾向は顕著です。で、新たな「国家神道」を創るためには、まず仏教と神道の違いを明確にせねばなりません。そこで明治政府は1868年に「神仏分離令」（「神仏判然令」ともいいます）を布告しました。これは神社にいる仏教僧たちを還俗させ、神社に仏像を神体とすることを禁じたものです。

　じつをいえば、明治政府がこの神仏分離令を出す200年前に、すでに1666年に会津藩・水戸藩・岡山藩においては、神仏習合をしている神社と寺院を分離する政策がとられています。また、3藩とも、約半数の寺院を破却しました。そして幕末になると、とくに国学の影響の強い地方においては、神仏分離政策が進行していたのです。したがって、明治政府はこのような動きを加速させ、また全国化したことになります。

　注意してほしいのは、明治政府が出したのは「神仏分離令」であって、仏教と神道の差別を明確にする意図のものです。もちろん、その先には「国家神道」の創設という目論見はありますが、その段階に

💬 What was the "movement to abolish Buddhism"?

The fundamental policy of the Meiji government was to nationalize Shintō. In this case, Shintō was not Yamatoism but State Shintō. Perhaps it would be more accurate to say that rather than nationalizing Shintō, the Meiji government's intent was to create from scratch a new "State Shintō."

However, as we have seen thus far, over a long period of history, Shintoism and Buddhism had formed a harmonious whole. That tendency was particularly prominent within Yamatoism. So, in order to create a new "State Shintō," it was first necessary to make a distinction between Buddhism and Shintoism. To do this, in 1868 the Meiji government issued the Edict for the Separation of Shintō and Buddhism. This edict returned Buddhist priests serving at Shintō shrines to secular life and prohibited shrines from making Buddhist images into objects of worship.

To tell the truth, two centuries before the Meiji leaders issued the edict, by 1666 in Aizu, Mito and Okayama domains, policies were in effect to separate shrines and temples which had fused the two religions. Moreover, in all three domains half of the temples were demolished. During the Bakumatsu period, the closing days of the Tokugawa government, especially in areas where the influence of National Learning was powerful, policies for separating Buddhism and Shintoism were making headway. Consequently, the Meiji government's efforts speeded up the process and made it into a national undertaking.

Please note that what the Meiji government issued was an edict separating the two religions, with the intention of making a clear distinction between them. Of course the eventual intention was to establish "State Shintō," but at that particular stage

CHAPTER 7 MODERN TIMES 189

おいては仏教を弾圧しようとする意図はありません。しかし民衆のほうでは、江戸時代の檀家制度によって仏教寺院からさんざんに痛めつけられていたので、この「神仏分離」ということを「仏教排斥」といったふうに受け取りました。そして寺院を破却したり、仏像や経典、そして伽藍を焼却したりしました。それで、このような動きを、

――廃仏毀釈――

と言います。この廃仏毀釈の運動の激しかった地域は、薩摩藩・松本藩・高山藩・津和野藩や伊勢の神領、隠岐や佐渡などでした。

Q❸ 「国家神道」について説明してください。

「国家神道」というのは、明治維新のあと、明治政府が国民を国家の都合に合わせてうまく操縦するために、急遽捏造した「宗教」です。もちろん、これは本物の宗教ではありません。国家権力が勝手に国民に押し付けたものであって、表面的には宗教の様相を持たせてはいますが、実質はニセモノ宗教にほかなりません。

すでに述べたように、1868年に明治政府は「神仏判然令」を出して、神社から仏教的色彩を拭い落とし、全国の神社を直接国家の支配下に置き、中央集権的に再編成する方針を打ち出します。これは「神道国教化政策」と呼ばれているものです。

そして1870年には「大教宣布」の詔が出され、天皇をトップにいただく国家神道が「大教」の名前で全国民に強制されることになりました。全国の神

the intent was not to suppress Buddhism. However, because they had suffered continuously under the *danka* (parishioner) system of the temples during the Edo period, the commoners took this "separation of Shintoism and Buddhism" as "anti-Buddhism." They demolished Buddhist places of worship, and reduced Buddhist images, sutras and temple buildings to ashes. This movement, therefore, is referred to as the "movement to abolish Buddhism." This anti-Buddhist movement was particularly fierce in Satsuma, Matsumoto, Takayama and Tsuwano domains, in the estates belonging to Ise, and in such places as Oki and Sado.

66 Would you please explain "State Shintō"?

"State Shintō" was a hastily concocted "religion" created after the Meiji Restoration by the Meiji government in order to manage and manipulate the citizens into conforming with the convenience of the nation. Needless to say, this is not a true religion. It was something the state authority of its own accord forced on the citizens of the nation. While on the surface it was given a religious tinge, essentially it was no more than a pseudo-religion.

As I have already said, the Meiji government issued the Edict for Separation of Shintō and Buddhism in 1868 and worked out a plan of action to remove the Buddhist coloring from all the shrines, place the country's shrines under the direct control of the state and centralize administrative power. This policy is referred to as measures to establish Shintō as the state religion.

In 1870 the Imperial Edict for Establishment of Shintō was issued, and State Shintō with the Emperor presiding at the top was forced on the entire citizenry under the name *Taikyō*

社は伊勢神宮を本宗（総本山）とするピラミッド型に組織されたのです。また、東京招魂社（のちの靖国神社）や湊川神社などの新しい神社もつくられ、天長節（天皇誕生の祝日）や神武天皇祭などの祝祭日が定められ、全国的に遙拝式が強制されるようになりました。

　この国家神道は、政府みずからが「宗教でない」と言っています。じつは明治政府が発布した「大日本帝国憲法」においても、信教の自由は保障されていました。それゆえ、国家神道が宗教であるなら、それを国民に強制はできません。そこで政府は、国家神道は宗教でないという強弁のもとで国民に押し付けたのです。ということは、政府みずからが国家神道がニセモノ宗教であることを認めていたのです。
　そして、この国家神道は、天皇を「現人神」（「現御神」ともいいます）とします。現人神とは生ける神であり、しかも完全無欠な存在です。本来、日本の神道（やまと教）の神は、前にも述べたように、まちがいをしでかすことが多く、欠点の多い神であるのです。
　ところが、この現人神はキリスト教のゴッドをモデルにつくられたもので、完全な存在でなければならないわけです。この点においても、国家神道は本来の神道（やまと教）を逸脱したものであって、ニセモノ宗教であることはまちがいありません。
　さらに、国家神道の聖典としてつくられたものに「教育勅語」があります。「教育勅語」は正しくは「教育ニ関スル勅語」といい、1890（明治23）年に発布されました。この「教育勅語」の思想は、日本の国民は普段は親孝行をしたり、夫婦が愛し合っ

(Great Teaching). All of the nation's shrines were organized into a hierarchy with Ise Shrine as the *Honsō* (*Sōhonzan*). New shrines such as Tōkyō's Shōkonsha (later Yasukuni Shrine) and Minatogawa Shrine were created, festival days such at *Tenchōsetsu* (celebrating the emperor's birthday) and *Jinmu Tennōsai* (celebrating the legendary first emperor) were established, and worship from a distance was enforced nationwide.

The government itself said that State Shintō is "not a religion." Even in the Constitution of the Empire of Japan, which was promulgated by the Meiji government, freedom of religion was guaranteed. Consequently, if State Shintō was a religion, it could not be forced upon the people. So the government, employing the sophistry that State Shintō was not religion, forced it upon the people. That is to say, the government itself admitted that State Shintō was a fake religion.

This State Shintō took the emperor to be a living deity (*arahitogami, akitsumikami*). *Arahitogami* is a living deity, an absolute perfect being. Properly speaking, the gods of Shintō (Yamatoism), as pointed out before, very often make mistakes and they are deities with many flaws.

However, this *arahitogami* was based on the model of the Christian God, so it had to be a perfect being. On this point, State Shintō deviated from the original Shintō (Yamatoism), and there is no mistake that it is a counterfeit religion.

Among the "sacred texts" composed to support State Shintō was the Imperial Rescript on Education (*Kyōiku Chokugo*). It was issued in the name of the emperor in 1890. The principles of the rescript said that the people of the country were to practice filial piety and that husband and wife were to live in harmony,

たりしていてもよいが、

《一旦緩急(イツタンカンキユウ)アレハ義勇公(ギユウコウ)ニ奉(ホウ)シ以テ天壌無窮(テンジヨウムキユウ)ノ皇運(コウウン)ヲ扶翼(フヨク)スヘシ》

ということです。すなわち、ひとたび国家の非常事態になれば（一旦緩急あれば）、親孝行もやめ、夫婦が愛し合うのもやめにして、進んで公共のために力を尽くし（義勇公に奉じ）、天皇の国家のために命を投げ出して奉仕せよ、と命じているのです。

宗教というものは、これまで何度も繰り返してきましたが、「人間らしい生き方」を教えるものです。けれども、国家神道の聖典である「教育勅語」が言っていることはそれとは反対で、人間らしい生き方をやめて、天皇の臣民（すなわち奴隷）としての生き方をせよ、というものです。その意味でも、この国家神道はいかにひどいニセモノ宗教であるかがお分かりになるでしょう。

なお、この国家神道は、敗戦直後の1945年12月15日にＧＨＱ（連合国軍総司令部）の指令によって解体させられました。すなわちＧＨＱは、いわゆる「神道指令」（正しくは「国教分離指令」）を発して、神社に対する特別の保護の停止、神道施設の公的機関からの撤去などを指示し、国家と神道との完全な分離を命じたのです。

そして翌1946年の元日には、昭和天皇みずからが、自分は現人神ではなく、ただの人間であるといった、いわゆる「人間宣言」をしました。天皇自身が、天皇を現人神とする国家神道を否定したのですから、結果的には国家神道はニセモノ宗教であったことを裏付けたわけです。

そして、国家神道の聖典ともいうべき「教育勅語」は、1948年6月19日に、衆議院と参議院にお

but also one should "in the case of an emergency, valiantly offer oneself to the State; in order to protect and sustain the prosperity of the Imperial Throne which came into being together with heaven and earth".

In other words, when matters of grave concern arise, it orders the setting aside of filial piety and conjugal harmony, rendering service for the public good of one's own accord, and rendering service to the emperor and the nation at the risk of one's life.

As I have frequently repeated, religion teaches how one ought to live as a human being. However, what the Imperial Rescript on Education, a "sacred text" of State Shintō, proclaims is just the opposite. It says that one should abandon the way of living of human beings and instead adopt the life of a subject of the emperor (that is, as a servant). From this, too, one can understand just how abominable the fake religion called State Shintō actually is.

Immediately following the defeat, on December 15, 1945, the GHQ of the Supreme Commander of Allied Powers (SCAP) ordered State Shintō dismantled. GHQ issued the Shintō Directive mandating the termination of special sponsorship and support of shrines, supported the removal of public functions from Shintō facilities and ordered the complete separation of state and Shintoism.

On New Years Day of the following year, Emperor Shōwa of his own accord made his "renunciation of divinity" speech, which proclaimed that he was not a "living deity" but an ordinary human being. Since the emperor himself contradicted State Shintō which had held that he was a divine being, he effectively substantiated the fact that State Shintō was a pseudo-religion.

The Imperial Rescript on Education, which should be called a sacred text within State Shintō, was officially rescinded by

いてその排除と失効の決議がなされました。日本人自身の手によって「教育勅語」は廃止されたのであって、占領軍による廃止ではなかったことを忘れないでください。

Q❹ 靖国神社とは、どういう神社ですか……？

　幕末から明治維新の戦乱において、多くの戦死者が出ました。その戦死者の霊を慰めるために、各藩は「旌忠社(せいちゅうしゃ)」などといった名称で招魂場を設けました。この招魂場がのちに「招魂社(しょうこんしゃ)」と改称されます。招魂社のうちには官営のものもあれば、私営のものもありました。

　さらに1939（昭和14）年になると各地にあった招魂社が整理されて、官私の別なく「護国神社」と改称され、各府県に1社が設けられました。

　一方、1869（明治2）年には、勅令によって「東京招魂社」が九段坂上に設立されました。そしてここに、各地の招魂社に祀られている戦死者の霊と、まだ祀られていなかった霊とを合祀しました。すなわち、1868年の鳥羽・伏見の戦いから翌年の箱館戦争にいたる戊辰(ぼしん)戦争の戦死者の霊を合祀したのです。

　さて、この東京招魂社が、設立10年後の1879年に抜本的に改革され、別格官幣社(べっかくかんぺいしゃ)に列せられて「靖国神社」と改称されました。

the Lower House and Upper House of the National Diet on June 19, 1948. Significantly, it was the Japanese themselves, not the Occupation forces, who abolished the rescript.

❝ What sort of shrine is Yasukuni?

A large number of people were killed in the disturbances of war between the last days of the Tokugawa and the restoration of imperial rule. To console [慰める] the spirits of the war dead, each domain established a memorial site with such names as "shrine of the loyalists." Eventually those shrines were renamed *shōkonsha*, meaning a Shintō shrine dedicated to the spirits of those killed in war. Of these, some were under government management and others were under private management.

In 1939 these memorial shrines in each locale [地方] were reorganized, renamed "Gokoku Shrine" regardless of whether they were managed by the government or other parties, and one shrine was constructed in each prefecture.

Meanwhile, in 1869 by imperial ordinance [布告] the Tōkyō Shōkonsha was constructed in Kudan. In this shrine, the souls of the war dead enshrined at *Shōkonsha* throughout the country were enshrined together with the souls of those who had not been enshrined elsewhere. That is, it enshrined the spirits of the war dead from the 1868 battle at Toba Fushimi, the Battle of Goryōkaku in Hakodate and the Boshin Civil War.

In 1879, ten years after it was completed, the Tōkyō Shōkonsha underwent a fundamental reorganization. Ranked together with the special-status national shrines, its name was changed to Yasukuni Shrine.

一般の神社は内務省の管轄下にありますが、この靖国神社は陸・海軍省と内務省の３省で管理運営されました。

　もっとも運営の主導権は陸軍省が持ち、内務省は神官の人事に関する権限しかもっていません。また天皇や皇族はしばしば靖国神社に行幸・行啓しました。

　では、いかなる目的で靖国神社が設立されたのでしょうか？　だいぶ辛辣な表現になりますが、靖国神社は日本の軍国主義と密接な関係を持った神社です。
　そもそも人間は、国民（国家に従属する人間）である前に「自由な人間」です。しかし、近代日本の国家は国家神道をつくり、日本人の全員を臣民（天皇に従属する人間）に変え、国家に奉仕する人間にしてしまったのです。

　そして、その臣民を兵士にし、その生命を奪ってしまいます。それが戦死者です。しかも、戦死した人間（死者）を遺族に返還せず、なおも国家の管理下に置こうとしたのが、靖国神社に象徴される、
　　──英霊──
　の思想です。
　戦死者は靖国神社に祀られることによって英霊（すぐれた人の霊魂）となることができる。
　そう教えておけば、戦死者の遺族は安心できます。その安心を与えることが、靖国神社の大きな機能であったと思われます。

Ordinary shrines fall under the jurisdiction of the Home Ministry, but Yasukuni Shrine was managed and administered by three ministries: the Army Ministry, the Navy Ministry and the Home Ministry.

Leadership in management of this shrine was taken by the Army Ministry, and the Home Ministry only had jurisdiction over personnel matters related to the priests. The emperor and members of the Imperial family every so often paid visits to the shrine.

For what purpose was Yasukuni Shrine established? It may be harsh to put it this way, but Yasukuni Shrine had an intimate connection with Japanese militarism.

By nature, before they are citizens (human beings subordinated to the state), humans are first and foremost "free human beings." However, the modern Japanese state created State Shintō, turned the entire people of the country into "subjects" (human beings subordinated to the emperor) and made them human beings who served the nation.

It made these subjects into soldiers and took their lives. These are the ones called "war dead." Moreover, the ideology of "spirits of the departed war heroes," symbolized by Yasukuni Shrine, not only would not return the deceased, who had been killed in war, to their families, but even attempted to keep them under the control of the state.

By enshrining them in Yasukuni Shrine, the war dead become "souls of the departed war heroes."

If one teaches this, then the bereaved families of those killed in war can rest at ease. Providing this peace of mind was considered a major function of Yasukuni Shrine.

Q❺ だとすると、神道はすべて国家神道になってしまったのですか？

　神道の国教化によって、国家神道が成立しました。この国家神道は国家の保障・支援を受けます。そのかわり、国家神道は「宗教」ではないとされていますから、独自の教義・教学を説くことはできません。ただ天皇の臣民として生きることだけが教えられていました。

　ところが、明治時代に、こうした国家神道のあり方に不満を持った人たちがいました。彼らは、それぞれの独自の教義を布教するために、国家神道から分派・独立して、仏教やキリスト教などと同じ「宗教」としての神道を形成しました。それが、

　　——教派神道（宗派神道・宗教神道）——

　です。明治政府によって公認されたものが13あったもので、これを「教派神道十三派」と称します。

　その名称だけを列挙しておきます。

　　——神道大教（たいきょう）・黒住教（くろずみきょう）・神道修成派（しゅうせいは）・出雲大社教（いずもおおやしろきょう）・扶桑教（ふそうきょう）・実行教（じっこうきょう）・神道大成教（たいせいきょう）・神習教（しんしゅうきょう）・御嶽教（おんたけきょう）・神理教（しんりきょう）・禊教（みそぎきょう）・金光教（こんこうきょう）・天理教（てんりきょう）——

66 If that was the case, did all Shintoism become State Shintoism?

By the establishment of Shintoism as the national religion, State Shintō was created. State Shintō received protection and support from the national government. In exchange, because State Shintō was not held to be a religion, it could not preach unique doctrines or teachings. It only taught that one should live as a proper subject of the emperor.

However, in the Meiji period there were some who were discontent with the situation in State Shintō. In order to propagate their individual respective doctrines, they broke off from State Shintō and established branches of Shintō just like the "religions" of Buddhism and Christianity.

These are the authorized denominations of religious Shintō called "sectarian Shintō." The Meiji government recognized what came to be called the "thirteen Sectarian Shintō sects."

They are comprised of the following:
Shintō Taikyō, Kurozumikyō, Shintō Shūseiha, Izumo Ōyashirokyō, Fusōkyō, Jikkōkyō, Shintō Taiseikyō, Shinshūkyō, Ontakekyō, Shinrikyō, Misogikyō, Konkōkyō, and Tenrikyō.

終章

日本人は宗教アレルギー

Q❶ 再び最初の質問に戻ります。
日本人は**無宗教**だと言われています。
本当にそうなんですか？

　序章においてわたしは、日本人は「国家神道」への反発の故に宗教アレルギーに罹ってしまった、と指摘しました。宗教に対して猛烈なアレルギー反応を起こし、そのために宗教嫌いになってしまったのです。宗教嫌いだから無宗教になるのです。そのことをもう一度、総括的にまとめておきます。

　さて、何度も繰り返しましたが、わたしは宗教というものを、「人間らしい生き方」を教えるものだと定義しています。ところが、明治政府が捏造したニセモノ宗教である国家神道は、人間らしい生き方を教えるどころか、逆に、現人神と規定された天皇にだけ忠誠を誓い、その天皇の臣民（という名の奴隷）となって生きる生き方を全国民に強制しました。国民はそのような生き方を義務教育の学校において徹底的に叩き込まれます。

　もっとも、明治時代はまだ国家神道の形成期・宣伝期であって、無理矢理の強制といっても、どこか余裕がありました。だから、歌人の与謝野晶子

FINAL CHAPTER

The Japanese Religious Allergy

> **Returning again to the first question, it is said that Japanese do not believe in religion, but is that true?**

In the introductory chapter, I pointed out that Japanese developed an allergic reaction to religion out of resentment against State Shintō. This caused an intense allergic reaction to religion as a whole and as a result the people came to dislike religion. Out of this extreme dislike of religion, they became *irreligious*. Let me now give an all-inclusive summary (要約) of this situation.

As I have frequently indicated, I define religion as that which teaches "a human way of living." However, State Shintō, the concocted fake religion created by the Meiji government, not only did not teach a human way of living, to the contrary it forced the people of the nation to pledge (誓う) their loyalty only to the emperor, who was said to be a living deity, and force the people to live their lives as subjects (that is, servants) of that emperor. The people had this way of living drummed (たたき込む) into them throughout compulsory (義務的な) education.

The Meiji period was the formative (形成の), disseminating (広める) period of State Shintō, and while its ideology (考え方) was forced on the people, there was still some margin (ゆとり) allowed. Therefore, the poet Yosano

(1878–1942) は、1904（明治34）年に「君死にたまふことなかれ」という反戦詩を発表しています。いや、反戦詩をまだ発表することができたのです。その詩は、

> あゝをとうとよ君を泣く
> 君死にたまふことなかれ
> 末に生まれし君なれば
> 親のなさけはまさりしも
> 親は刃をにぎらせて
> 人を殺せとをしへしや
> 人を殺して死ねよとて
> 二十四までをそだてしや

といったものでありました。

じつはこのとき、与謝野晶子の実弟は、同年に始まった日露戦争に従軍していました。それで彼女は弟の身を案じて詩を詠んだのです。彼女はこう言っています。親は子どもに人殺しをせよとは教えなかった。互いに殺し合って死ぬのが名誉だなんて、いったい誰が言ったのか。あなたは商家の生まれである。商家に生まれたあなたには、旅順が陥落しようがしまいが、関係がない。母はめっきり白髪が増えた。あなたの新妻は、あなたの無事を祈って泣いている。だから弟よ、決して戦死してはならない、と。

考えてみてください。これが人間としてのあたりまえですね。人間らしい生き方とは敵を殺すことではありません。晶子は、その人間らしい生き方を言っているのです。

もちろん、晶子のこの詩に対する非難・攻撃はありました。晶子を「乱臣賊子（国を乱す臣と親にそ

Akiko (1878–1942) was able to publish an anti-war poem in 1904 (Meiji 34) titled "I wish you not to die, my dear". The times were such that she could still get such poetry published. The poem begins:

> "O dear brother, I weep for you.
> I sincerely wish you not to die.
> Born as the last son in our family,
> our parents' love for you exceed all.
> How could they make you take up a sword,
> and tell you to kill someone?
> Did they bring you up to the age of twenty-four
> only to kill others and die yourself?

As it happened, Yosano Akiko's younger brother was sent to the front during the Russo-Japanese War, which began that same year. She composed the poem out of concern for her brother and the following is what she says. Our parents did not raise us to kill others. Who taught us that there is honor in killing another and dying? You were born in a merchant family, so what difference could it make to you whether Port Arthur (Lushun) falls. The gray hairs on our mother's head have increased noticeably. Your wife cries, praying for your safety. So, dear brother, you must not die in this war.

Consider this. This is only natural for a human being. Living as a human being should live does not mean killing enemies. Akiko is talking precisely about this human way of life.

Needless to say, this poem by Akiko was criticized and attacked. Some people denounced her as "a traitorous subject."
糾弾する　　　　　　　　国賊的な

むく子の意）と弾劾する人もいました。しかし、晶子に対して暴力は加えられていません。それは、まだ国家神道が未発達だったからです。

けれども、国家神道が大きく発達し、それが国民の肉体も精神をも支配するようになった昭和の時代には、晶子のような発言をすれば、国家権力によってその人間は殺されてしまいます。だから人々は、国家神道の熱心な信者にならざるを得ませんでした。少なくともその振りをせねばなりません。人々はこのニセモノ宗教の犠牲になったのです。

その結果、日本人は宗教にうんざりするようになりました。なにせニセモノ宗教に対しては、ホンモノ宗教であるはずの仏教もキリスト教も文句を言わないどころか、積極的に尻尾を振っていたのですから、宗教なんて信用できないと思うのはあたりまえです。ただし、誤解しないでください。わたしは国家神道と闘った人は1人もいなかったと言っているのではありません。そういう人もいたのですが、ほんの少数だったのです。

ともかく、日本人が宗教嫌いになり、宗教アレルギーになったのは、この国家神道のせいです。その結果、現在にいたっても日本人は、むしろ宗教に無関心なのが良心的な態度だと考えているように思われます。

Q❷ しかし、戦後の日本には新興宗教が雨後の筍のように誕生しましたね。

"新興宗教"とは、文字通りには新しく成立した宗教教団ですが、この呼称は既成宗教の側から軽蔑的

But Akiko was not subjected to violence. That was because State Shintō was not yet fully developed.

But in the Shōwa era, when State Shintō developed greatly and came to control the bodies and souls of the people, anyone who dared to utter a remark like hers would have been murdered by the authority of the state. Therefore, people were forced to become ardent believers in State Shintō. At the very least, they had to pretend to be ardent believers. They fell victim to the pseudo-religion.

Accordingly, the Japanese became sick and tired of religion. After all, not only did Buddhism and Christianity, which were supposed to be true religions, not raise objections to the pseudo religion, they even actively curried favor with it, so it was entirely natural to think that religions could not be trusted. Please do not misunderstand me. I am not saying that there was no single person who stood up against State Shintō. Some did, but they were all too few in number.

In any case, the fact that Japanese came to dislike religion and developed an allergy to it was the fault of State Shintō. As a consequence, even today the Japanese would seem to think that indifference to religion is rather a conscientious attitude to take.

> **However, after World War II, didn't "New Religions" spring up like mushrooms after a rain?**

The "New Religions" (*shinkō shūkyō*) are literally religious organizations that were newly established, but in many cases

に使われることが多く、最近は"新宗教"という呼称のほうが使われています。

歴史的には、それぞれの時代に新宗教が成立しています。たとえば鎌倉時代に成立した浄土宗、浄土真宗、臨済宗、曹洞宗、日蓮宗などは、その時代においては新宗教でありました。また、江戸時代の末から明治の初期に成立した黒住教、天理教、金光教なども、その時代の新宗教です。さらに明治中期には大本教が新宗教として成立し、第１次大戦の時期にめざましく発展しました。しかし、それらの諸宗教を、今日では「新宗教」と呼ぶ人はあまりいないでしょう。

今日、新宗教といえば、だいたいにおいて20世紀になって新しく形成された教団を指すと思えばよいでしょう。そのうち主要な教団を紹介します。

大本教……大本教の開祖の出口なおは、生活苦にあえぎながら金光教に帰依していました。そして1892年に突然神がかりし、数千冊にのぼる「お筆先」の執筆を始めます。この「お筆先」がのちに『大本神諭』としてまとめられました。出口なおは、その後、金光教の布教師となります。彼女は金光教の軒を借りて布教活動を続けていましたが、のちには金光教と決別して大本教を独立させました。さて、この大本教を発展させたのは、上田喜三郎（のちに王仁三郎と改名）です。彼は出口なおの神がかりの言葉を理論化し、その信頼を得ました。そして、1900年には出口なおの後継者となる５女のすみと結婚し、教義の体系化、教団の組織化を進

that designation has been used in a pejorative sense by the established religions, so nowadays the term *shin shūkyō* (a more neutral form of "new religions") is used.

Historically, new religions have been established throughout the various eras. The Jōdo, Jōdo Shin, Rinzai, Sōtō and Nichiren sects—all founded in the Kamakura period—were at one time "new religions." Religions like Kurozumikyō, Tenrikyō and Konkōkyō—founded between the late Tokugawa and early Meiji periods—were considered "new religions" in their own day. In the mid-Meiji period, Ōmotokyō was established as a "new religion" and it developed remarkably around the time of World War I. However, nowadays few people refer to these as "new religions" (*shin shūkyō*).

In the present day, for the most part, "new religion" (*shin shūkyō*) can be taken as referring to those religious organizations that were formed during the 20th century. Let me introduce the major groups.

Ōmotokyō—Deguchi Nao, founder of Ōmotokyō, was originally a believer in Konkōkyō as she struggled just to get by in life. In 1892 she suddenly began to experience divine possession and began writing several thousands of *"Fudesaki,"* which were later collected in *Ōmotoshinyu*. Deguchi later became a propagator of Konkōkyō, and continued under those auspices until she broke away and established Ōmotokyō. The one who developed Ōmotokyō was Ueda Kisaburō (who later took the name Onisaburō). He brought theory to the divine utterances of Deguchi Nao and gained her confidence. After marrying Deguchi Nao's successor and fifth daughter Sumi, he systematized the doctrines and promoted its organization. Fired with enormous resentment toward the capitalists and landowners

めました。王仁三郎は、戦争によって富を増大していく資本家や地主に対して激しい憤りを燃やし、日本の庶民を不幸に追いやる戦争に反対します。このような大本教の姿勢は、当然のことながら政治権力からの弾圧を受けます。1921年には第1次弾圧、1935年には第2次弾圧を受けました。第2次弾圧はひどいもので、政治権力によって京都府の綾部と亀岡にある大本教の本部施設はダイナマイトによって爆破されてしまったのです。しかし、第2次世界大戦後は、大本教は「愛善苑」と改称し、王仁三郎を苑主として出発し、一貫して戦争反対を叫び、平和運動を展開し続けています。なお、現在の教団名は「大本」です。

霊友会……日蓮宗系の新宗教教団。法華経の信者であった久保角太郎と霊能力者の小谷喜美が中心となって、1925年に発足させた「大日本霊友会」に端を発します。その教義は法華信仰と祖先供養を結合させたもので、第2次世界大戦中に東京を中心に発展しました。すでに戦前に、孝道教団や思親会、立正佼成会などが分派独立し、戦後になって妙智会、仏所護念会、妙道会などが独立しました。

創価学会……初代会長の牧口常三郎が、のちに第2代会長となる戸田城聖とともに結成した「創価教育学会」がその前身です。牧口は、日蓮宗の一派である日蓮正宗の信徒であったところから、その日蓮正宗の信徒の組織として発足しました。第2次世界大戦中に弾圧を受け、牧口は獄死しましたが、戦後

who had made fortunes as a result of war, Onisaburō opposed the war which had driven the common people into such miserable conditions. Naturally this stance on the part of Ōmotokyō brought suppression from the political authorities. The first crackdown came in 1921 and the second in 1935. The latter was particularly severe, ending with the headquarter facilities of Ōmotokyō at Ayabe and Kameoka in Kyōto Prefecture being blown up with dynamite by the political powers. However, following World War II, Ōmotokyō changed its name to *Aizen-en*. Starting off with Onisaburō as its head, it consistently called for opposition to war and has continued its movement for peace. The name of the organization is currently Ōmoto.

Reiyūkai—A new religious organization of the Nichiren sect variety. The organization came into being as Dai Nippon Reiyūkai in 1925, centering on Kubo Kakutarō, a believer in the Lotus Sutra, and Kotani Kimi, a psychic medium. Its doctrines consolidated faith in the Lotus Sutra and the veneration of ancestors, and during World War II it developed primarily in the Tōkyō area. Prior to the war, splinter groups including Kōdō Kyōdan, Shishin-kai and Risshō Kōseikai went independent, and following the war Myōchi-kai, Bussho Gonen Kai and Myōdō-kai became independent.

Sōka Gakkai—Founder Makiguchi Tsunesaburō and Toda Jōsei organized the Value-Creating Educational Society (Sōka Kyōiku Gakkai), precursor to the present organization. Makiguchi was an adherent of Nichiren Shōshū, a denomination of the Nichiren sect, and his group began as an organization of other Nichiren Shōshū believers. The group was suppressed during

に創価学会として復活し、戸田の指導によって大きく発展しました。戸田の死後（1958年）は池田大作が総務として統率、1960年には池田が第3代会長に就任しました。創価学会は1955年から地方議会へ、翌年から参議院へ議員を送り始めていましたが、池田は1964年に公明党を結成し、1967年の総選挙では25名を当選させました。

　　立正佼成会……法華経信仰系の新宗教。霊友会の信者であった庭野日敬が、天理教信者であった長沼妙佼とともに、1938年に「大日本立正交成会」を結成したのが最初です。教団名は1948年に「立正交成会」、1960年に「立正佼成会」と改称されます。第2次世界大戦後、東日本を中心に急成長して大教団となりました。先祖供養を重んじ、懺悔道に精進し、菩薩道に邁進することを教えています。

　　ＰＬ教団……御木徳一によって創設された「ひとのみち教団」が、1946年に徳一の長男である徳近によって改名、再建された教団です。教団名のＰＬは、「パーフェクト・リバティ（完全な自由）」の頭文字をとったもの。「人生は芸術である」「人の一生は自己表現である」「自己は神の表現である」を信条とします。

　　世界救世教……大本教から分派した新宗教。教祖の岡田茂吉は、観音が彼の体内に入り、観音力を得

World War II and Makiguchi died in prison, but after the war, revived [復活する] under the name Sōka Gakkai, the group made major advances under Toda's leadership. Upon Toda's death in 1958, Ikeda Daisaku became director of general affairs and in 1960 assumed [引き受ける] office as the third president (*kaichō*) of the organization. Beginning in 1955 Sōka Gakkai began supporting candidates for local assemblies [議会] and in the following year, for the House of Councilors [参議院] of the National Diet. In 1964 Ikeda formed Kōmeitō (the Clean Government Party), and in the general election of 1967, 25 of its candidates were elected to office.

Risshō Kōseikai—A new religion based on the teachings of the Lotus Sutra. Founded in 1938 by Niwano Nikkyō, a member of Reiyūkai, and Naganuma Myōkō, a believer in Tenrikyō, its first form was the Dai Nippon Risshō Kōseikai. It took the name Risshō Kōseikai in 1948, and changed one character but kept that name in 1960. Following World War II, the group experiences rapid growth, particularly in eastern Japan. It emphasizes ancestor veneration [崇拝], penitence [さんげ] and devotion to others, and striving to follow the path of the bodhisattva.

PL Kyōdan (The Church of Perfect Liberty)—Founded by Miki Tokuharu as Hito no Michi Kyōdan (the Way-of-Man Organization), in 1946 Tokuharu's eldest son Tokuchika changed the name and reorganized the group. It took the first letters of "Perfect Liberty" for the name PL Kyōdan. It takes as its principles "Life is art," "The whole life of the individual is self-expression," and "The individual is a manifestation of God."

Sekai Kyūseikyō (The Religion for the Salvation of the World)—A new religion which branched off from Ōmotokyō. Founder

たとして、みずからメシヤ(救世主)と称しました。そして1935年に「大日本観音会」を設立します。1947年には「日本観音教」と改称し、1952年に「世界救世教」と再改称されました。

Q❸ 1995年にはオウム真理教事件もありましたが……。

　1995年3月20日、東京の地下鉄で、12人の死者と約5500人の重軽症者を出すサリン事件が発生しました。捜査によってこの事件はオウム真理教(その後、教団名は「アレフ」に改称されました)が関与していることが分かり、またこの教団はそれ以前にもさまざまな事件を起こしていることが分かりました。

　しかしながら、オウム真理教事件については、まだ裁判が進行中ですので、わたしの論評は加えないでおきます。

Okada Mokichi believed Kannon entered his body and he obtained the powers of Kannon, referring to himself as "Messiah." In 1935 he founded the Dai Nippon Kannonkai (Japan Kannon Society), which became Nihon Kannonkyō in 1947 and was reorganized as the World Messianity Church (Sekai Kyūseikyō) in 1952.

❖ What was the Aum Shinrikyō Incident in 1995 all about?

On March 20, 1995, the Sarin Incident occurred in Tōkyō's subway system killing 12 and slightly or seriously injuring approximately 5,500 others. According to the investigation, Aum Shinrikyō (later renamed Aleph) was found to be involved, and it was further discovered that the organization was responsible for various earlier incidents.

Because the court case involving the Aum Shinrikyō Incident is still in progress, I will refrain from commenting further.

最後に

　最後に、ちょっと言っておきたいことがあります。それは、日本人はまったくひどい宗教音痴だということです。

　日本人は、宗教というものが「平和」なものだと思っています。宗教者というのは、温厚でおとなしい人だと思います。だが、それは、いわゆる「葬式仏教」と呼ばれる、去勢された仏教・宗教しか知らないためです。実際に宗教は、もっと荒々しいものです。荒々しくなければ、わたしたちを教え導くことはできません。

　それは、たとえば前の質問のときに出てきた大本教を考えてください。大本教は戦争に反対して、権力から弾圧を受けています。いま現在の時点に立つと、大本教の主張は正しかったと思います。しかし、大本教が弾圧された時点においては、日本の庶民の大半が大本教を「邪教」と思ったはずです。政治権力に尻尾を振って戦争を賛美している仏教教団こそが正しい宗教であり、権力に反対する宗教を邪教と判断したのです。

　また、キリスト教を考えてください。キリスト教のイエスは、世を騒がせる犯罪者として、ユダヤ教徒に殺されたのです。ユダヤの民衆は、ローマ総督ピラトが、
「反逆罪で殺人犯であるバラバか、イエスか、どちらか１人を釈放してやる」
と言うのに対して、バラバを釈放し、イエスを処刑せよ、と選択しました。彼らにとってイエスは処刑されて当然の「悪人」だったのです。

IN CLOSING

In closing, I would like to make a comment. That is, I believe that the Japanese people have absolutely no sense when it comes to religion.

The Japanese seem to think that religion is a matter of "peace." They think that religious leaders are gentle, calm people. But that is because all they know is the neutered Buddhism and religion, the so-called "funeral Buddhism." In actuality, religion is a tougher entity. Unless it is harsh and fierce, it cannot teach and guide us.

Think for a moment about Ōmotokyō which was taken up in the previous section. Because Ōmotokyō opposed the war, it was suppressed by the authorities. When we look at it from the present day, we realize that the case that Ōmotokyō made was the correct one. However, at the point when Ōmotokyō was suppressed, the majority of ordinary Japanese must have looked upon its views as heresy. They saw the Buddhist organizations that flattered the government powers and glorified the war as the correct religions, judging any religion opposed to the authorities as heresies.

Consider Christianity, too. Jesus was killed by the Jews because he was stirring up the people. When the Roman governor Pilatos asked the crowd of Judeans whether they wanted him to release the treasonous murderer Barabbas or Jesus, they called for Barabbas to be released and Jesus to be executed. To them, Jesus was a criminal who should be killed.

ということは、宗教というものは、見方によっては恐ろしいものなのです。その人が社会のどの階層にあるかによって、宗教の見方は変わってきます。権力側に立てば、権力を批判する宗教は「邪教」になるでしょう。権力によって虐げられている民衆の側に立てば、権力に味方する宗教のほうが「邪教」です。また、虐げられた民衆からすれば、権力を批判してくれる宗教こそを待ち望んでいるのです。

　そして、そういうことを考えようともしない日本人は、まことに宗教音痴です。この宗教音痴を早く匡正しないことには、日本人はまたしてもニセモノ宗教に誑かされてしまいます。わたしはそれを憂えています。

What this means is that depending on one's point of view, religion can be a frightening thing. Depending on one's position within society, one's religious point of view may change dramatically. If one stands on the side of authority, then any religion which opposes that authority becomes "heresy." If one stands on the side of people who are oppressed by authority, then the religion that takes sides with authorities becomes "heresy." From the perspective of the oppressed peoples, it is the religion which criticizes authority that is eagerly sought.

That the Japanese do not so much as begin to consider this fact shows just how hopeless they are when it comes to understanding religion. Unless this lack of a sense of religion is corrected soon, the Japanese will repeatedly succumb to pseudo religions. This leaves one deeply apprehensive.

ひろ さちや　Hiro Sachiya

1936年、大阪市生まれ。東京大学文学部インド哲学科卒、同大学院博士課程終了。気象大学校教授を経て、現在、大正大学客員教授。仏教を中心とした宗教問題や人間の生き方にかんして幅広い執筆・講演活動を行っている。著書は『釈迦とイエス』『ひろさちやの般若心経88講』『仏教 はじめの一歩』『「狂い」のすすめ』など500冊を超える。

ジェームス・M・バーダマン　James M. Vardaman

1947年、米国テネシー州生まれ。ハワイ大学でアジア研究専攻、修士。1976年来日し、いくつかの大学で教鞭をとったのち、現在は早稲田大学教授。著書に『アメリカ南部』『わが心のディープサウス』『アメリカ日常生活のマナーQ＆A』『よく使う順 英会話フレーズ』、編書に『アメリカの小学生が学ぶ歴史教科書』など多数。

ひろ さちやの英語で話す日本の宗教 Q＆A
Hiro Sachiya Talks about Japanese Religion

2010年6月8日　第1刷発行

著　者　　ひろ さちや
翻訳者　　ジェームス・M・バーダマン

発行者　　大村数一
発行所　　株式会社ジャパンブック
　　　　　〒189-0001　東京都東村山市秋津町 3-17-85
　　　　　電話　042-313-3555
　　　　　http://www.japanbook.co.jp

印刷所　　豊国印刷株式会社
製本所　　豊国印刷株式会社

定価はカバーに表示してあります。
乱丁・落丁本は、ジャパンブックまでお送りください。
送料小社負担にてお取替えいたします。
本書の無断複写（コピー）は著作権法上での例外を除き、禁じられています。

Copyright © 2010 by Hiro Sachiya, James M. Vardaman
Printed in Japan
ISBN 978-4-902928-10-5

日本の文化を、やさしい英語で面白く話す！

EJ対訳ブックス

ビジネスに、国際交流に、
ホームステイに、留学に！
——日本を説明するときの
欠かせない1冊です。

スピーク・ジャパン！
英語で話す日本のすべて

緯度だけを合わせて、大西洋に日本列島を浮かべたら、どんな位置にどんな大きさで入るか想像できますか？——日本の政治・経済から衣食住にいたるまで、必須のデータをおさえながらも、目からウロコの面白知識がイッパイつまっています。外国の人たちとの会話をもりあげてくれる1冊です。

内池久貴＋JapanBook編集部[著]　マイケル・ブレーズ[訳]
定価：本体1600円＋税　ISBN978-4-902928-06-8

なぜ、日本人は？
答えに詰まる外国人の質問178

■ なぜ、みんな専用のお茶碗とお箸を持っているのですか？
■ なぜ、日本のご飯には味がついていないのですか？
■ なぜ、力士は褌一本で恥ずかしくないのですか？
■ なぜ、家に入るとき靴をぬぐのですか？
■ なぜ、大人も漫画を読むのですか？　etc.
——こんな外国人の難しい質問にキッパリ答えます。

内池久貴＋Office Miyako[著]　マイケル・ブレーズ[訳]
定価：本体1500円＋税　ISBN978-4-902928-05-1

英語で話す日本史
やさしく、面白く、分かりやすく

十七条憲法は日本国憲法と同じようなもの？ 古事記と日本書紀、なぜ同じような歴史書が同じ時期に作られた？ 清少納言と紫式部、会ったことはある？「ガリバー旅行記」のガリバーは日本に来て踏み絵をさせられそうになった。いったいどうして？
——バーダマン教授がやさしい英語で面白く語る日本史。

ジェームス・M・バーダマン[著] 高橋豊子[訳]
定価：本体1500円＋税　ISBN978-4-902928-08-2

カラー版

村上祥子の
英語で教える日本料理

外国の人に日本料理を教えるってタイヘン。海外ではなかなか材料が手に入らないし、計量の仕方も違います。それに、いくらおいしく作っても、日本料理がそのまま海外の人に気に入ってもらえるとは限りません。海外経験の深い村上祥子さんが、外国人にも「わっ、おいしい！」と言わせるレシピを教えてくれます。

村上祥子[著]
定価：本体1800円＋税　ISBN978-4-902928-04-4

英語で教える
折り紙コミュニケーション

折り紙は世界の人と仲良くなる最高のコミュニケーションツール。たった1枚の紙からハサミも糊も使わずに、いろいろなカタチを作り出す技術に、外国の人たちは目を見張ります。でも作り方を説明するのは難しい。できるだけ分かりやすく、やさしく、楽しく説明する英語にコダワった折り紙の本です。

山口　真[著]　マイケル・ダイニンガー[訳]
定価：本体1400円＋税　ISBN978-4-902928-07-5

「アメ小」コンビ、10万部突破！
「英語の教養」を身につける本

対訳

アメリカの小学生が学ぶ 歴史教科書

本書はバージニア大学のE. D. ハーシュ教授が編纂したアメリカの小学生用教科書から、アメリカ史の部分を抜粋したものです。やさしく書かれていますが、ネイティブ感覚いっぱいの英語で、物語のように面白くアメリカ史を読むことができます。アメリカ人との会話をもりあげてくれる1冊です。

ジェームス・M・バーダマン（早稲田大学教授）
村田 薫（早稲田大学教授）[編]
定価：本体1500円＋税
ISBN978-4-902928-00-6

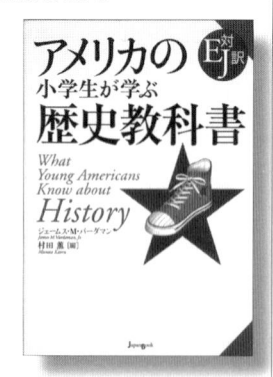

本書の特長

1 「これが歴史教科書？」と思わせるドキュメンタリー・タッチの記述。
2 日本人が身につけるのにふさわしい英語がここにあります。
3 アメリカの歴史的出来事を英語でどういうのかが分かります。
4 真珠湾攻撃、原爆投下、ベトナム戦争――アメリカ人の考え方が分かります。
5 アメリカ人との会話がはずむトリビアの宝庫です。

対訳

アメリカの小学生が学ぶ 国語・算数・理科・社会 教科書

ここでは国語・算数・理科・社会の教科の中から、英語として知っておきたい単語や常識を網羅しました。小学校の教科書とはいっても、日本人にとってはテーマ的にも、英語的にも盲点になっている、日常の英会話に必要な新しい知識がいっぱいです。大学の教科書にも続々採用されています。

ジェームス・M・バーダマン（早稲田大学教授）
村田 薫（早稲田大学教授）[編]
定価：本体1600円＋税
ISBN978-4-902928-02-0

テーマは

- ユダヤ教、キリスト教、イスラム教、ヒンドゥー教、仏教、儒教の成り立ちと教義
- ギリシャ神話と『イリアス』『オデュッセイア』、『アーサー王と円卓の騎士団』『ラーマーヤナ』などの物語。etc.

英語は

- 国語・算数・理科・社会、各教科必須の基礎的な英語表現がいっぱい。
- 『大の月、小の月』『円周率』『年号』などをどう覚えるか？　etc.